SPIRITUAL DIMENSIONS
OF MENTAL HEALTH

Judith Allen Shelly, Sandra D. John & Others

InterVarsity Press
Downers Grove
Illinois 60515

InterVarsity Press is the book-publishing division of Inter-Varsity Christian Fellowship, a student movement active on campus at hundreds of universities, colleges and schools of nursing. For information about local and regional activities, write IVCF, 233 Langdon St., Madison, WI 53703.

Distributed in Canada through InterVarsity Press, 860 Denison St., Unit 3, Markham, Ontario L3R 4H1, Canada.

Biblical quotations, unless otherwise indicated, are from the Revised Standard Version of the Bible, copyrighted 1946, 1952, © 1971, 1973.

Cover photo: Robert McKendrick

ISBN 0-87784-876-9

Printed in the United States of America #9756663

Library of Congress Cataloging in Publication Data
Shelly, Judith Allen.
    Spiritual dimensions of mental health.

    (The Spiritual perspectives in nursing series)
    Includes bibliographical references.
    1. Psychiatric nursing—Religious aspects—
Christianity. I. John, Sandra D. II. Title.
III. Series. [DNLM: 1. Christianity—Nursing texts.
2. Nursing, Psychiatric. WY 160 S759]
RC440.S485   1983   610.73'68   83-12769
ISBN 0-87784-876-9

17 16 15 14 13 12 11 10 9 8 7 6 5 4 3 2
95 94 93 92 91 90 89 88 87 86 85 84

*To Grace Wallace, without whose faith
and encouragement this project would
never have happened.*

Foreword

It took only a few semesters of teaching psychiatric/mental health nursing before I began to identify some recurring themes when students expressed their feelings about the psychiatric nursing experience. As students anticipated starting the semester, they would often tell me, "I'm scared." That statement was usually followed by "but I'm excited." However, it became apparent that the feeling of fear predominated, and I began to wonder why.

Perhaps one reason is that in psychiatric/mental health nursing, more than any other clinical area, the philosophical component is evident. Students are forced to examine who they are and what they believe. The issues are behavioral and conceptual rather than procedural and technical. The central task is relational—the person of the helper with the person of the helped. All the props are removed and there is no place to hide. Our human vulnerabilities are often challenged. As one student told me, "What's to say that the balance couldn't be tipped for me as well?"

In discussions with nursing colleagues, other professionals and even some lay persons, pertinent questions often arise about the spiritual dimension of mental health:

What is a spiritual need?

How is it different from an emotional/psychological need?

Can spiritual needs be assessed?

How can spiritual needs be met?

Doesn't religion sometimes make people sick?

Christian students seem to echo the "I'm scared" theme even more loudly than other students, for they have additional fears and concerns.

Is psychology compatible with Christian faith?

How can I tell my clients about God's love for them?

Can Christians become mentally ill? If so, does that mean they have lost their faith?

How can I work with colleagues who ridicule my faith?

My students are not unique in their concerns. Nurses across the nation are asking similar questions. Nurses Christian Fellowship is committed to helping students find answers to those questions. In 1977 a workshop, "Wholeness versus Fragmentation: A Christian Perspective on Mental Health" was developed in the West, spearheaded by task-force member Sandi John. In 1979 Southern California NCF Staff developed a Bible-study guide entitled "Mental Health: A Biblical Perspective," and proposed the formation of a task force to produce further materials on the spiritual dimensions of mental health.

In October 1980 Nurses Christian Fellowship began the project with funding from the Maclellan Foundation and the J. Howard Pew Memorial Trust. Judith Shelly, Associate Director for NCF Resources, and I collaborated in planning to bring Christian leaders in psychiatric/mental health nursing together to share their expertise. The task force first met in April 1981 at Fellowship Deaconry, Liberty Corner, New Jersey. A year of developing working papers, compiling a bibliography and further planning followed.[1] The task force reconvened in April 1982. We evaluated, revised and challenged one another's work, then went back to writing until this manuscript was completed. In the process, numerous articles for nursing journals were also produced. They are now beginning to appear in print.[2]

Before, during and after the task force meetings, it was my singular privilege to plan and work closely with Judith Shelly. I also count it an immense privilege to have worked with each task force member. We were a covey of "all chiefs and no Indians," but an overwhelming spirit of humility, openness and mutual encouragement prevailed at our meetings and in our written communications. The presence of the Holy Spirit in our midst was clearly evident. The process through which our task was completed was one of the most poignant experiences of my life.

This book would not have been possible without the commitment, hard work and personal sharing of each task force member. Judith Shelly and I would like to express our very special gratitude to each participant: Ann Bacon, Verna J. Carson, Ramona Cass, Joyce Samhammer Hays, Judith L. Jensen, Sandra D. John, Norine Kerr, Sidney Langston, Barbara Nelson, Barbara Olin, Shirley Pilster-Pearson, Mertie Potter and Cheryl Webb.

We would further like to express appreciation to the support committee of the Eastern Regional Advisory Work Committee of Nurses Christian Fellowship—Erna Goulding, Mary Kay Sauder and Edith Martin—who provided generously for our physical and emotional needs as we met together. Janet Reinbrecht, Lois and Al Faro, and Francis Covert braved traffic, bad weather and hectic schedules to coordinate transportation for task-force members. Finally, we are grateful for the Sisters at Fellowship Deaconry who encouraged and prayed for us as we met in their facilities.

Diana A. Krikorian, R.N., M.S.Ed.
University of Delaware

Section 1
What Is Mental Health?

1
Mental Health: A Personal Struggle
Judith Allen Shelly

The Seventh Floor was mysterious and a bit foreboding. No one ever saw it, beyond the view from the elevator, until junior year, except the patients, of course, and the people who worked there. On the first day of psychiatric nursing clinical experience, we took a tour of the place and received our key to the locked wards. The key was important. It was the concrete division between *them* and *us*. Whenever you doubted your own sanity you could look at the key and tell yourself, "I'm okay."

We needed that reminder, because during our psych nursing experience the dividing line between the mentally ill and the "normal people" became fuzzier and fuzzier. Often we suspected that we really belonged on the other side of that fuzzy line, and we feared being found out. To relieve the pressure on ourselves we began to diagnose our classmates and practice our newly learned skills on one another.

Pat: Sue and I went for a walk after class to see the fall leaves. The trees in the park are beautiful!

Jan: The trees?

Pat: Yes, and we saw a little squirrel sitting on his haunches eating a walnut. He was so cute!

Jan: Cute?

Pat: Good grief, I can't even talk to you. All you do is repeat my words. I sure will be glad when you get done with that psych course!

After we studied Freud's interpretation of defense mechanisms and learned that excelling at academic pursuits was one way of redirecting sexual drives, we put signs on our doors saying "Subliminating" when we studied. It was intended to be humorous, but an underlying sense of doubt in our own mental health precipitated our behavior.

We feared a lot of things in psych nursing. Everyone knew that last semester Marcia came home from clinical with a black eye after a patient struck her. The man who had killed an aide in the state hospital just got out of the locked ward last week. His roommate kept making sexual overtures and exposing himself whenever a student entered his room. A young woman who had been admitted with an overdose of drugs, including LSD, seemed normal at times, but would unexpectedly begin to hallucinate and scream uncontrollably, grabbing out for anyone who was close by.

We also feared that we would be ridiculed for our faith. Those fears, however, did not materialize. We had gentle and wise instructors who respected our Christian beliefs and values. They supported us in our own faith and helped us examine the distorted religious ideas of our patients as part of the disease process. I cannot remember ever being told that a patient was sick because of his religion. I have since learned that my experience was unusual, and that many students face strong opposition to their faith.

We feared physical harm and being ridiculed for our faith, but these fears were mild compared with the overwhelming fear of facing ourselves. One patient in particular brought this fear to the surface.

Lynn was a twenty-year-old junior nursing student from another university. During her psychiatric nursing experience she began to hallucinate. She saw little "ice people" who told her to do things. One day the ice people told her to take a knife and make slits all over her body to let them out. Her roommate found her in a pool of blood in their dorm room. After the wounds healed she was transferred to our hospital for psychiatric treatment.

Lynn became very religious after she entered the hospital. She read her Bible and prayer books constantly. Formerly a Baptist, she decided to convert to Roman Catholicism and became deeply fascinated with the sacrifice of the Mass.

The psychiatrist in charge of Lynn's treatment decided that family therapy would be helpful. There were many deeply rooted problems and a history of sexual abuse, but when her parents and brothers arrived for therapy sessions they looked so normal, so much like our own families. Our identification with Lynn was strong.

We spent quite a bit of time in group conferences discussing Lynn. We wondered whether what happened to Lynn could happen to us. She had been mentally healthy enough to be admitted to the nursing program and had made excellent grades in all her nursing courses. We learned that Lynn would probably not be readmitted to her school, and we wondered how much of our own fears and anxieties we dared reveal before we too would be asked to leave. We were confused by the way her interest in spiritual things seemed to increase in direct proportion to the severity of her illness. We struggled with whether Christians could become mentally ill, and if so, whether that means they have lost faith. Lynn forced us to look at ourselves, our fears, our own personal wounds from the past, our relationships and our faith with new insight. She helped us break through the *them* and *us* mentality to a supportive working together toward wholeness. She made us very much aware of the tenuous nature of mental health.

The anxieties of students beginning their psychiatric/mental health nursing experience may be strong, even overwhelming. For many students it is a time of opening old wounds; for others it is a time of increasing self-assurance, but for each it is an opportunity for healing and a lifelong move toward wholeness to begin.

Now let's change scenes. It has been over sixteen years since I met Lynn and struggled with my student anxieties. I am sitting in a room with twelve other women. We are the Nurses Christian Fellowship Mental Health Task Force. All of us have advanced degrees in psychiatric/mental health nursing, counseling, psychology or social work. Our first meeting the night before was awkward. Most had traveled long distances. We were tired, a little shy, preoccupied with our own concerns, feeling inadequate for the task; yet each was sure that everyone else "had it all together."

Today, however, a special sense of rapport and openness permeates the atmosphere, and we proceed through the agenda with a sense of expectancy. As we work through the intellectual task of defining mental health and describing how each has integrated spiritual care into nursing practice, an amazing thing begins to happen. Personal problems and struggles are laid out before the group, honestly and humbly. The women in the group begin to minister to one another. Spontaneous prayer, counseling, singing, and mutual support are interspersed with the tremendous volume of work being produced. At one point in the discussion one of the Task Force members says, "Didn't most of us go into this field because we had nagging doubts about our own mental health?"

Yes, Christians do have emotional problems. Mental health is always a relative concept. Each of us lives within a continuum of mental health and mental illness. Many factors, including our faith, help to keep us closer to the healthy range of the continuum; however, a crisis, a long-term hostile environment, physical illness or spiritual distress can work together with other factors to push us in the direction of mental illness.

Before we define mental health further, we need to clarify what we mean by spiritual health, for the two concepts are frequently confused. According to the definition developed by a special sub-committee after the 1971 White House Conference on Aging, "Spiritual well-being is the affirmation of life in a relationship with God, self, community and environment that nurtures and cele-brates wholeness."[1] In many ways, spiritual well-being parallels mental health. From a Christian perspective, though, spiritual well-being can exist only when a person is in a dynamic, personal relationship with God through faith in Jesus Christ. When we speak of spiritual needs we are speaking specifically of the factors necessary to establish and maintain that dynamic, personal rela-tionship with God.[2] Ideally, if a person were in perfect relationship with God, that person would also be a specimen of perfect mental health; however, none of us has achieved perfection. Physical, spiritual and mental health are interrelated because we are inte-grated beings. We cannot isolate one dimension of personality and treat it apart from the other dimensions.

We will be focusing on that dimension of our being which we call *mental health.* In the process we will look at the interrelation-ship of the spiritual and, at times, the physical dimensions with the mental/emotional. We will examine our own mental health as well as provide some guidelines for caring for others. Primarily, this will be a book of sharing. The first Task Force meeting began with the overwhelming sense that the Holy Spirit was among us, doing his work in our innermost being. Each of the authors has experienced mighty upheavals and deep healing in his or her life. Each of us has been made greatly aware of our own weakness and the amazing power of God. We are grateful that God's power is made manifest in our weakness.

2
What Is Human? A Context for Defining Mental Health

Judith Allen Shelly and Sandra D. John

W hew! I survived another day in the zoo. I sure will be glad when this psych rotation is over. I'm tired of dealing with all these crazies." Jennifer looked distraught as she joined the other members of her clinical group for dinner. Her comment spurred the others to elaborate on Jennifer's perception of psychiatric nursing.

"You wouldn't believe what this weirdo I'm working with is like. She thinks she's Joan of Arc. Apparently she also thinks that Joan doesn't wear clothes."

"Well, at least Joan of Arc talks. How am I supposed to do a verbatim on a creature who just squats in a corner grunting and groaning?"

"The place really is a zoo, isn't it? These people aren't even human. It's spooky."

What *does* it mean to be human? The question stretches beyond psychiatric nursing. Is the comatose, severely brain-damaged individual who is being kept alive by life-support systems human? Is a fetus human? Throughout history *humanity* has been defined according to the convenience of those in power. American slaves could be bought and sold, used and abused because they were considered less than human. Hitler could justify his extermination of Jews by his limited view of what was human. Abortion and euthanasia can be advocated only in the context of a restricted view of humanity. The biblical view of humanity does not allow us the privilege of defining what is human by our own whims and convenience.

The psalmist marveled: "What is man that thou art mindful of him, and the son of man that thou dost care for him? Yet thou hast made him little less than God, and dost crown him with glory and honor" (Ps 8:4-5). We are created by God and given great meaning, purpose and self-worth simply by virtue of our relationship with God. That value does not change with physical, mental, moral or even spiritual impairment. Consider David's relationship with Saul in the Old Testament (1 Sam 17—2 Sam 1).

Saul was the first king of Israel. David was a shepherd and part-time soldier who came to Saul's attention when he killed Goliath, the Philistine. Their relationship was strained from the beginning because of Saul's avid jealousy of David. David nevertheless maintained a deep respect for Saul and attempted to soothe his troubled spirit by playing the lyre for him. In return, Saul tried to kill David with his spear.

As Saul's emotional condition deteriorated, his attempts to kill David became more relentless and bizarre. David was forced continually to run for his life. On two occasions David found himself in an ideal position to kill Saul. Both times he refused, saying, "The LORD forbid that I should do this thing to my lord, the LORD's anointed" (1 Sam 24:6), and "Do not destroy him; for who can put forth his hand against the LORD's anointed, and be guiltless?"

(1 Sam 26:9). David continually tried to reason with Saul and to treat him with dignity and respect. When Saul was finally killed in battle, David mourned in bitter anguish, recalling the days of Saul's glory.

David was able to see Saul as a person of great worth in the eyes of God, in spite of his pathological behavior. He did not consider him a mere madman who was out to get him, but "the LORD's anointed." The Scriptures assert that each person is anointed to serve as a priest and a child of the King (1 Pet 2:4-10). C. S. Lewis described our responsibility to humbly honor even the most unlovely:

> It is a serious thing to live in a society of possible gods and goddesses, to remember that the dullest and most uninteresting person you talk to may one day be a creature which, if you saw it now, you would be strongly tempted to worship, or else a horror and a corruption such as you now meet, if at all, only in a nightmare. . . . There are no *ordinary* people. You have never talked to a mere mortal. . . . Next to the Blessed Sacrament itself, your neighbor is the holiest object presented to your senses.[1]

The woman who thinks she is Joan of Arc, the man who sits autistically in a corner, and every other patient on the psychiatric unit are holy—created and set apart by God for his glory. But something has gone wrong.

Humanity and Sin

It is no longer fashionable to speak of sin, but it is the common condition of the human race. Christians often feel guilty about believing that sin is a problem. We have been taught to be nonjudgmental. But is it not strange that we are afraid to own our beliefs in public when all around us we are confronted by crime, the threat of war, child abuse, spouse abuse, broken marriages, anger, bitterness and alienation? Psychiatrist Karl Menninger believes that by avoiding the subject of sin we have made the problem worse.[2] If there is no sin, why do we all feel so guilty? If we cannot acknowledge sin, then there is no opportunity to experience forgiveness. The Scriptures do not dance around the issue. Romans 3:23 boldly declares, "All have sinned and fall short of the glory of God."

The question we must address is, What is sin, and what is its relationship to mental illness? Simply stated, sin is turning away from God and putting the self in God's rightful place. It is our natural tendency to put ourselves first. The effects of sin are evident in our lives and clearly outlined in the Scriptures:

> For although they knew God they did not honor him as God or give thanks to him, but they became futile in their thinking and their senseless minds were darkened. (Rom 1:21)
>
> Now the works of the flesh are plain: fornication, impurity, licentiousness, idolatry, sorcery, enmity, strife, jealousy, anger, selfishness, dissension, party spirit, envy, drunkenness, carousing, and the like. (Gal 5:19-21a)

But what is the relationship of sin to mental illness? Some, such as pastoral counselor Jay Adams, would go so far as to say that mental illness is not illness at all but *sin*. [3] Most Christian therapists would not go to that extreme. While the effects of sin force us to contend with suffering, death, injustice, despair, human perversion, alienation and overwhelming feelings of guilt, it is not necessarily personal sin which causes mental illness. Mental illness can result from any number of environmental, chemical, relational, biological and hereditary factors, as well as from personal choices or lack of choices. We can no more say that all mental illness is the result of sin in a person's life than we can claim that all physical illness is the result of an individual's sin.

But the problem of sin is very real in many forms of mental illness. The teen-ager who has a psychotic break after many years of being sexually abused by her father is suffering the effects of sin. The Vietnam veteran who is still reliving the horrors of war certainly can witness to the inhumanity of sin. The woman with an involutional depression whose husband left her for a younger woman, and whose son is in jail for selling drugs, knows the reality of sin, and she knows that she is guilty of having contributed to the situation. Most of these people feel immobilized by sin and consumed with guilt. Quoting Scripture and telling them how to behave will not solve their problems.

Sin is not something we can overcome by ourselves. It is only in a dynamic personal relationship with God and his people that we can gain any power over sin. Romans 5:1-2 tells us:

Since we are justified by faith, we have peace with God through our Lord Jesus Christ. Through him we have obtained access to this grace in which we stand, and we rejoice in our hope of sharing the glory of God.

God's grace, appropriated through faith, is the means by which we can overcome the effects of sin. Faith is an important ingredient in the healing process in mental illness, but it is not the only ingredient. Healing usually takes place in a long-term process of therapy, which may include counseling, medication, a change of environment and treatment of physical ailments.

Treating the Whole Person

Joe was a normally loving husband and father with a violent temper. He had been in counseling for six months but seemed to be making no progress. At certain times he could not control his temper. He would beat his wife and daughter without provocation. Both he and his family were frightened because his bouts of violence were so unpredictable. One evening Joe came home from work with five different flavors of ice cream. The family enjoyed an ice cream splurge after dinner, trying each flavor. It was a good evening with healthy family interaction—but within hours Joe was violent again. Suddenly it dawned on Alma, Joe's wife, that each episode of temper was preceded by eating ice cream or drinking milk. Laboratory tests revealed that Joe had a rare allergy to milk. When milk products were removed from his diet, his "mental illness" was cured.

Nancy was a conscientious nurse. Her unit had a reputation for being the best surgical floor in the hospital. She was respected for being a fair and caring head nurse. Everything in Nancy's life seemed to be going right. She was engaged to be married to a man she deeply loved. She was making straight A's in the graduate courses she was taking three evenings a week. She was active in her church and had started a Bible-study group among nurses at the hospital. Then she was admitted to the hospital with a bleeding ulcer.

George was an elder in his church. He was never known for a pleasant personality, but he prided himself on his exemplary life. When George's son, Jeff, came home from college and said that he was moving in with a girlfriend, George threw Jeff out of the house and vowed never to speak to him again. His blood pressure skyrocketed, and within a month he had a myocardial infarction. Jeff called their pastor and said he wanted to visit his father in the hospital but was afraid that George would refuse to see him. The pastor suspected that George's inability to forgive Jeff was related to his hypertension. He began talking with George about his rela-tionship with his son.

A physical disorder with an emotional manifestation, a fear of failure internalized as a somatic condition, a spiritual sickness which precipitated a life-threatening physiological response—these all demonstrate that we are complicated people. It is not possible to treat a mental illness without taking the whole person into consideration. Diet, exercise, intake of alcohol or tobacco or other drugs, and general physical health deeply affect the way we think and feel. Our relationships with others help to shape our self-concept, our goals and values, and our approach to life. Our education and life experiences also help to shape our world and life views. Our relationship with God gives ultimate meaning and purpose to life, a basic sense of security and belonging, and the ability to love and forgive. An unhealthy relationship with God can create serious physical and emotional disorders.

The psalmist discovered this long ago: "When I declared not my sin, my body wasted away through my groaning all day long. For day and night thy hand was heavy upon me; my strength was dried up as by the heat of summer" (Ps 32:3-4). No amount of psychiatric treatment or vitamins or proper hydration was going to heal the psalmist of his depression, malnutrition and dehydration until his basic spiritual need to repent and be forgiven was met. But it may have taken months of counseling to discover that unconfessed sin was his problem, and his physical deterioration certainly was not conducive to clear thinking. As the above case studies show, the basic problem is not always apparent. We must be extremely careful not to prejudge a person's pathology.

What Is Mental Health?

Mental health or illness cannot be adequately considered without looking at the whole person, but for the purposes of this book we will attempt to focus primarily on the mental/emotional dimension.

Mental health is a nebulous term which defies definition. Any definition of mental health is value-laden. The criteria you might use to determine whether a person is emotionally stable may not be valid in another culture—or even to another person in your own community. As we attempt to determine a person's level of wellness, we bring our own values and perceptions into the assessment. Basic beliefs and assumptions undergird every definition of mental health. In proposing a Christian definition, we draw our presuppositions from the Bible and a biblical view of humanity. We assume that optimal mental health can only be maintained when a person is in dynamic, personal relationship with God, because we believe that God created us that way.

Mental health, from a Christian perspective, is a state of dynamic equilibrium characterized by hope, joy and peace, in which positive self-regard is developed through the love, relationship, forgiveness, meaning and purpose resulting from a vital relationship with God and a responsible interdependence with others.[4]

Dynamic equilibrium means that there are daily ups and downs, but overall a steady state is maintained. It also implies that mental health is not an all-or-nothing situation, but a broad range of emotions and mental processes. Persons who are generally healthy sometimes experience temporary depressions. Delusional clients sometimes have periods of profoundly rational thinking. Mental health is an atmosphere, a tone or a quality along a continuum of several dimensions. A person in a state of dynamic equilibrium will be able to cope with crisis, be flexible, make adjustments to life's changes and resolve problems and conflicts. The healthy person does not always feel hopeful, loving, joyous and peaceful, but does find that life is basically characterized by these attitudes.

Proper positive self-regard comes from a vital relationship with God. Psychologist Paul Meehl states, "If man were in the proper relationship to God, he would not feel condemned (either by God, his fellows, or himself); he would derive the richest, truest, and most satisfying meanings, because in all things he would be God-oriented."[5] Knowing that we are created by God in his image, redeemed and forgiven by him, we can accept ourselves. We can recognize our uniqueness and our basic worth, not needing to compare ourselves with others. We can take responsibility for our own decisions, feelings, thoughts and behavior, and examine ourselves critically and nondefensively. We can be vulnerable without feeling threatened, taking both positive and negative feedback from others. With hope for the future, we can set goals and direction for life. We can express our emotions without hurting ourselves or others.

Mentally healthy individuals are able to give and receive love, and to be intimate with others without losing their own identity. They are able to forgive others and accept forgiveness when they have wronged another. When necessary they may confront another person, express anger and say no. They affirm other people, but can also give constructive criticism. They are grounded in a community which provides the stability to enable them to risk change and growth.

The concept of time figures heavily in the mental health of a person. The past is over, forgiven, healed. It is not forgotten or repressed, but remembered realistically with its joys and sorrows. It does not block freedom of choice in the present. The present is lived freely with joy, reality, meaning and purpose. The future is approached with hope and confidence, both for life on this earth and for the afterlife. St. Paul shows a healthy view of the future when he says, "I do not consider that I have made it my own; but one thing I do, forgetting what lies behind and straining forward to what lies ahead, I press on toward the goal for the prize of the upward call of God in Christ Jesus" (Phil 3:13-14).

Mental health encompasses the feelings, thoughts and behavior of a person in relationship to God, self and others in the past, present and future. A mentally healthy person is a spiritually healthy person who lives in a dynamic personal relationship to God and other people. However, our worth before God is not determined by our mental health any more than it is determined by our physical health. We share a common humanity with the mentally ill and the mentally healthy. Because we are human, we all share a need for love, relationship, forgiveness, meaning and purpose.

What does it mean to be human? It means being created and loved by God. It means being made in God's image to serve the lofty purposes designed for us by our Creator. It means sharing in the awful effects of sin, being sinners ourselves who need forgiveness. It means being complicated, integrated persons who function simultaneously in the physical, emotional, mental and spiritual dimensions. We each function in fluctuating degrees of strength and weakness, health and illness, but we remain human —even into eternity—and, regardless of our physical, mental or spiritual condition, each person is worthy of dignity, respect and comprehensive care by other human beings.

3
Toward a Psychology of Believing
Judith Allen Shelly

Ruth knocked on Betty's door as she was completing her application to a graduate program in psychiatric/mental health nursing. Betty shared her enthusiasm with her friend, but Ruth just shook her head.

"I don't see how you can go into psychiatric nursing. It is nothing but atheistic humanism. It seems to me that being a Christian and being in psych are totally incompatible," Ruth declared.

Betty looked surprised. "I don't see any conflict between Christianity and psychiatry," she said. "After all, Jesus was the best psychiatrist who ever lived. I think the Bible supports all the major psychological theories, too."

Ever since the time of Sigmund Freud there has been tension

between psychology and Christianity. Many therapists view Christianity with suspicion or even derision. Many Christians view psychiatry with fear and distrust. At the same time our society has gradually been deeply influenced by the self-actualizing philosophies of humanistic psychology. The influence is so subtle and so pervasive that most Christians do not recognize it. A plethora of Christianized pop psychology books flood the market. Many merely take a psychological theory and proof-text it with Scripture, giving the appearance that it is a contemporary expression of the gospel. Hence we are faced not only with a tension between Christianity and psychology, but also with a tension between Christians who hold widely differing views of psychology.

Two problems confront us as we try to evaluate psychology from a Christian perspective. The first is prejudice. There is the prejudice of Christians who fear "godless humanism" and the prejudice of mental health practitioners whose only contact with Christianity is the pathological distortion of faith seen in their clients. In both cases education is necessary. We need to begin to listen to one another.

The second problem is the lack of evaluative skills among Christians. We need a process by which to systematically appraise psychological theories from a biblical perspective. Theories differ widely from one another. Some are even diametrically opposed to each other. But each theory is based on the careful observations and subjective experiences of serious scientists. None can be offhandedly dismissed. Each has some value and some degree of truth, so each must be considered individually to determine whether various aspects of it are compatible or incompatible with Christian faith.

Maslow and Rogers

One of the most influential theories in schools of nursing is Abraham Maslow's hierarchy of human needs, which proposes that needs must be met in an ascending order. Needs for food, shelter, security and belonging must be met before a person is able to progress to the higher needs of love, meaning and spirituality.[1] Maslow builds on the premise that human beings have an essential biologically based inner nature, which is not intrinsically evil but is either neutral, pre-moral or positively good. He sees the goal of healthy growth as "self-actualization," which he considers the "single ultimate value for mankind, a far goal toward which all men strive." He maintains that

> these propositions affirm the existence of the highest values within human nature itself, to be discovered there. This is in sharp contradiction to the older and more customary beliefs that the highest values can come only from a supernatural God, or from some other source outside of human nature itself.[2]

Evil behavior, according to Maslow, is the result of ignorance about interpersonal relationships or a reaction to bad treatment. He believes it will disappear with self-actualization.

Another psychological theorist who greatly affects nursing curricula is Carl Rogers. Rogerian listening is perhaps the most widely taught (and abused) technique in psychiatric nursing. Carl Rogers introduces his book *On Becoming a Person* by stating that experience is his highest authority, and upon that experience he builds his working theories. In working with clients over the years he has determined that all persons have a basically positive direction. He feels that even persons who are cruel and destructive have "strongly positive directional tendencies" at the deepest level. He sees life as constantly in the process of "becoming," and his role as therapist to be that of giving others "the permission and the freedom to develop their own meaningful interpretation of their own experience."[3]

As a nursing student, I never thought of questioning these theories or considering whether they were consistent with my faith in Christ. I accepted them with equal weight as the Krebs cycle and the germ theory. Psychological theory has become an integral part of our culture and our nursing education. We often accept it as if it had divine authority or at least unquestioned scientific validity. Modern psychology has made significant contributions to our society, but it remains *theory*, not *facts*. As Christians we must learn to be discerning about what we accept. We must resist the temptation to dichotomize our professional knowledge and our Christian faith; we must also resist the temptation to integrate the two spheres by proof-texting and compromise. The way to begin is by holding each psychological theory up to biblical understandings of human nature, the meaning and purpose of life, and the dynamics of human relationships.

A Comparative Evaluation

We have already outlined some of the major biblical concepts about human nature: We are integrated physically, mentally and spiritually and created in the image of God (Gen 1:27; Deut 6:4). We are fully alive only when we are in relationship with God (Gen 2:7; Rom 8:10). We are also born with a natural tendency to sin, which plagues us all our lives (Rom 7:23).

Most psychological theories agree that we are integrated beings; however, few are concerned about the image of God or the spiritual dimension. For example, Maslow sees the need for God as immature. Rogers, in overthrowing his conservative Christian upbringing, credits his conversion to humanism as the most significant factor in gaining his personal independence.[4]

Many personality theories present persons as being basically good. Maslow sees persons as having an essential biologically based inner nature which is intrinsically either neutral, pre-moral or positively good. Rogers views people as having "strongly positive directional tendencies." The apostle Paul illustrates the Christian view of the human condition when he states, "I do not understand my own actions. For I do not do what I want, but I do the very thing I hate" (Rom 7:15). That is hardly a "strongly positive directional tendency."

Thus, we are faced with a dilemma if we accept these theories in total as foundations for Christian nursing. Basic spiritual needs cannot be met if we do not recognize a person's need for God. The need for forgiveness cannot be met if the problem of sin is not acknowledged. However, many aspects of Maslow's and Rogers's theories are consistent with the Christian faith. There is a basic recognition of the value of the person and a commitment to helping the person become free from the crippling effects of a low self-image.

In some cases we may be dealing with different frames of reference. For instance, what does Maslow mean when he calls a person's inner nature "good"? Is he saying what we are hearing? Maslow is concerned with what is good for the person according to his own personality structure; he is not interested in applying any absolute moral standard by which to reorient the person. However, the Christian focuses on God and our relationship to him. Because of our self-centeredness and rebellion against God, we know we are not good. But self-centeredness is a virtue to the humanistic psychologist, and God is a human invention. Maslow and Rogers maintain that persons, if properly facilitated, will naturally move toward goodness and fulfillment, but the Christian must assert that we can move in a positive direction only through the grace of God. Both psychology and Christianity seek to guide people in a positive direction, but the definition of that positive direction may differ.

Next, let's compare views about the meaning and purpose of life. According to the Bible human beings were created by God to worship and serve him (Is 43:7; Ps 100:3-4; Eph 2:10). A person's proper goals are already set by God. Christians believe that it is only in the pursuit of these goals and purposes that a person will find fulfillment. Romans 1:21-25, in speaking of those who deny God, puts the point across strongly:

> They became futile in their thinking and their senseless minds were darkened. Claiming to be wise, they became fools. . . . Therefore God gave them up in the lusts of their hearts to impurity, to the dishonoring of their bodies among themselves, because they exchanged the truth about God for a lie and worshiped and served the creature rather than the Creator.

It seems to be dangerous ground to glorify the self over the One who created that self, yet this appears to be the direction of some humanistic psychologists. Maslow designates self-actualization as the chief goal of human beings. Rogers restates the same position in different words. Christian faith does not negate the self; instead it requires us to see ourselves as we really are before God—sinners who are deeply loved by God. We cannot expect to achieve self-actualization apart from a dynamic, redemptive relationship with God.

Finally, let's look at understandings of personal relationships. The Christian concept of interpersonal relationships can be summed up by 1 John 4:11-12: "Beloved, if God so loved us, we also ought to love one another. . . . If we love one another, God abides in us and his love is perfected in us." The ability to love one's neighbor is dependent upon a relationship with God whereby that love is given to us. God intended us to live in loving relationship with one another, but it is only by his power that we can do so.

Maslow's research seems to have led him to an interesting conclusion in this regard. Because his self-actualized person finds little need for relationships, he may tend to become less responsible, especially in helping other people. As a corrective, Maslow appeals to a Zen Buddhist sense of "oughtness" in helping others.[5] He further concludes that Taoism leads to a higher form of objectivity and is useful in integrating the "healthy animal, material, and selfish with the naturalistically transcendent, spiritual, and axiological."[6]

Rogers shows insight when he makes his "general law" of interpersonal relationship dependent on "congruence." In other words, a good relationship is most likely to develop if the awareness, experience and communication of the persons involved converge.[7] From a Christian perspective, the need for congruence means that human love can only reach the limits set by our selfish nature. It must ultimately disappoint its object. Only Christian love, based on God's love for us, can transcend the need for congruence.

Reconciling the Differences

What is a Christian nurse to do with Maslow and Rogers? Some would dismiss them as "godless humanists" and see no validity in their work. Others seem to accept them without questioning, saying, "All truth is God's truth." But these fail to discern between truth and falsehood. Others make personal experience the ultimate authority: if it makes sense they believe it. In so doing they join Carl Rogers, who states: "Neither the Bible nor the prophets —neither Freud nor research—neither the revelations of God nor man—can take precedence over my direct experience."[8]

Experience can be a powerful teacher, but it is colored and shaped by the personal baggage we bring with us—our hopes and fears, our backgrounds and our prejudices. Observations and experiences in the realm of human nature cannot be constructed in a vacuum. Often we see just what we want to see. The problem in psychological theorizing is that the scientist must move beyond pure observation and attempt to find meaning in the experience. Students of human behavior must approach their field from some philosophical system in order to provide that sense of meaning. Maslow states the need for "religion with a small r."[9] Rogers retains many of the values of his Christian heritage, but redirects them into humanistic philosophy. A Christian must view the study of human behavior in the light of God's purposes as revealed in the Scriptures.

The observations made by psychological research cannot be merely discarded. They are not so much wrong as incomplete, or incorrectly interpreted. A person cannot become self-actualized without knowing the Creator who designed that self and who alone holds its fulfillment. To see mankind as basically good is naive—even a shallow observation of the world around us will witness to human corruption. However, to see human beings as valuable creatures is essential. Maslow and Rogers affirm human worth but twist the concept to say that our chief end is ourselves. According to Scripture, such a lifestyle leads to despair and futility. Only in realizing that we are created by God for himself can we find real meaning and purpose in life. The goal of most schools of psychology is to enable the client to enter into meaningful, constructive relationships. That is also one of the results of a healthy relationship with Jesus Christ. Psychology can give us some of the means by which to understand the dynamics behind broken relationships and alienation, but only God's love can supply the power by which true restoration and belonging can occur.

As Christians we may freely borrow from the discoveries of secular psychology, if we are able to put them into a framework based on God's revelation. The Word of God will not be disproven by experience and scientific investigation; it will only be affirmed. Where conflict arises, the concepts must be studied seriously in the light of the Scriptures. If disagreement persists after careful evaluation, the authority of Scripture must prevail for the Christian.

4
Interpretations of Wholeness
Judith Allen Shelly

'm not *just* a nurse, I'm a *whole person*," Polly told her room-mate. "When I get home from work, I'm certainly not going to a meeting with a bunch of nurses!"

Our society is obsessed with a passion for "wholeness." We do not want to be identified by the roles we play, nor do we want to be defined by our relationships. "I'm not Joe's wife or Susie's mother, I'm Beverly Johnson," a young woman screams. She has decided to divorce Joe and leave Susie with him, so she can go out in the world and find "the real me." Wholeness and self-fulfillment seem to be closely linked in popular thinking today.

Most nurses now view the client as a multidimensional person who is in dynamic relationship to other people and the environment. No good nurse would ever refer to a client as "the gall bladder in room 315" anymore. The focus on wholeness is also a focus on caring and compassion and on client participation in health care. It requires us to see a client as a person rather than a disease, and it demands a deeper involvement than mere physical care. To move away from the old definition of health as the absence of disease to a broader concept of "wellness" or "wholeness" forces us beyond the physical realm into the spiritual dimension. We cannot determine what it means to be whole without making philosophical and religious assumptions about the nature of humanity and the workings of the universe.

The concept of wholeness is not new. From the earliest recorded history health care has been viewed as a religious and community function. It was only in the glow of fairly recent medical wonders that the physical dimension was separated from the spiritual and mental aspects of personality. But unqualified acceptance of modern medicine's ability to cure every problem with drugs and surgery was short-lived.

First, we learned that medicine could not cure everything. Although many fearful diseases were eradicated or cured, other serious maladies increased or became more severe. Second, modern medicine demanded a major tradeoff in personal independence and responsibility. Instead of dying at home with dignity and peace in familiar surroundings, the person was taken to a frightening hospital room with restricted visiting hours, where death was held at bay for weeks and months by an assortment of tubes and machines. Third, the powerful effect of the emotions on the body became clearly evident. Stress was recognized as a potent factor in heart disease, hypertension and almost every other disease process. Finally, the spiritual dimension again became a respectable concern. If we are to view health as more than the absence of disease, if health means instead complete well-being, then there has to be something more than just physical and emotional equilibrium. After all, suicide continues to be a leading cause of death. People seem to require something to live *for*. The current focus on wholeness is an attempt to discover who we are and why we are here. It is basically a spiritual quest, often thinly veiled in scientific or philosophical terminology.

Wholeness in the Bible

Before looking at current concepts of wholeness, we need to establish a biblical frame of reference. Many holistic health advocates will accuse the Christian faith of perpetuating a body-soul dualism. This concept, however, came not from the Bible but from the Greek philosopher Plato. Platonism viewed the body and the material world as imperfect, transitory and shadowy. The spiritual realm was totally separate from the material, and was viewed as perfect, permanent and real. The superior spirit was housed in an inferior body of clay from which it longed to be released.[1]

The early church incorporated Platonic thought into much of its theology. Its vestiges can still be seen in some aspects of modern Christianity, but it is strongly contrary to the biblical view of human wholeness. Even Plato complained, "This is the great error of our day in the treatment of the human body: that physicians separate the soul from the body."[2]

Throughout the Old and New Testaments healing and salvation are synonymous. God is concerned with the well-being of the whole person. To speak of "spiritual healing" or "saving souls" apart from the healing of the whole person is not biblical. Salvation encompasses the concepts of ease, safety, cure, recovery, redemption, remedy, rescue and welfare.[3] It puts the whole person into relationship with God and frees us to fulfill the destiny for which God intended us. That destiny is to live in this world (Gen 2:7) and continue to live eternally with our Creator (Jn 3:16); it is to live in loving relationship to other people (Mt 22:39), to rule over creation (Gen 1:26; 2 Tim 2:12), and to praise God (Ps 8; Eph 1:12).[4]

Unique to the biblical view is the idea that the whole person is in *need* of salvation. We are unable to save ourselves. We are unable to be fully self-aware or self-fulfilled without the grace of the Creator God who loves us and gave his own Son to die for us. We believe that Jesus Christ is God and has a unique relationship with God the Father. We believe that the Holy Spirit is God, and though we may be filled with the Spirit, we can never become one with God, or be God. Our relationship with God is personal and dynamic, but it always remains the relationship of a creature to the Creator.

The material world is real and it is good. God created it for our use and responsible stewardship. Pain, disease, catastrophe, fear and anxiety are real. They are the result of the evil in the world which has been present since Adam and Eve succumbed to the tempter's promise, "You will not die. For God knows that when you eat of it your eyes will be opened, *and you will be like God,* knowing good and evil" (Gen 3:4-5, emphasis added).

The spiritual world is also real. God is at work in the world accomplishing his purposes (Rom 8:28). We can talk to him just like a child can approach a loving father. We don't need any mystical techniques or formulas; we can merely tell him about our anxieties and concerns and he hears us and answers us (Mt 6; Ps 34). When Jesus died on the cross for our sins he defeated Satan, but until he comes again in glory we have to contend "against the principalities, against the powers, against the world rulers of this present darkness, against the spiritual hosts of wickedness in the heavenly places" (Eph 6:12). There is a spiritual realm which, though it may not be perceived by the physical senses, is very real.

All this may seem like a rather tedious review of Christian theology, but it becomes extremely important when we try to evaluate current trends and concepts of wholeness. When it comes to world views and understandings of reality, Christianity does not claim to be just one understanding of the truth, but The Truth. One man who tried to merge his Christian faith with the philosophies of the East eventually had to reject Christianity because he realized that the two were incompatible. Few are that honest. He described Christianity as "uncompromising, ornery, militant, rigorous, imperious, and invincibly self-righteous."[5] Those are negative and uncomfortable terms, but if we insist on remaining orthodox in our beliefs we may be similarly accused. If we accept the "unique divine inspiration, entire trustworthiness and authority of the Bible,"[6] we must adhere to a world and life view which is not compatible with other religions or with many secular philosophies. We must make choices which will not necessarily put us in the mainstream of current trends and thinking.

Evaluating new philosophies of caring is not always easy. Terminology is often confusing or obscure. Underlying assumptions are not always clear. Approaches may be unconventional and go beyond the traditional confines of nursing practice. Part of the difficulty is the transitional state of nursing today. As nurses strive to become more independent and more respected as professionals, two trends have developed. One is the attempt to be increasingly scientific in our rationale; the other is the desire to redefine the health care hierarchy. Both are essentially positive goals, but both can lead to an assortment of questionable methods as well as to some that are highly constructive.

Many nurses show little discrimination in their adaptation of new concepts. Continuing education programs offer a potpourri of theories and philosophies which seem innovative and attractive. The Judeo-Christian frame of reference which formerly provided the foundation for philosophies of nursing is no longer the only perspective. Science is often wedded to philosophy. Christian nurses, often with very little training in philosophical thinking or Christian doctrine, are left to evaluate the acceptability of the concepts and methods.

Holistic Health

A Christian nursing instructor became concerned as she watched a man and woman lead a group of chronically mentally ill clients in "relaxation exercises." They told the clients to "close your eyes, be comfortable, breathe deeply, and sing this song with us." They explained the words of the song, which they sang in an Indian language, to mean, "I bow down to myself."

One of the clients asked, "Is this a religion?"

The woman replied, "No, just a way to relax."[7]

Relaxation exercises of many varieties are just some of the techniques employed by advocates of holistic health. The holistic health movement is a growing philosophy of health care which attempts to focus on wholeness and the whole person. Effie Poy Yew Chow, R.N., Ph.D., president of the East-West Academy of Healing Arts, defines holistic health as "a conceptual system and perspective of comprehensive health care which . . . embraces concepts of optimal well-being and disease prevention by investigating and implementing health care methodologies which address the person as a whole being and treat the person as a self-responsible unit within the framework of his or her psycho-physio-socio-cultural-spiritual relationship with the environment."[8] So far, that sounds compatible with a Christian view of the person. Chow then expands on her definition by citing the following concepts as basic to holistic health:

It deals with wellness rather than illness.

It adopts the philosophical and theoretical tenets of other cultural healing systems.

It functions on the theoretical basis of energy systems, acknowledging the premise of an existing universal, vital life force that has not yet been sufficiently explained or researched.[9]

Preventive health care is an admirable and necessary function of nursing. We have a responsibility to take proper care of our own bodies and to teach others about the importance of exercise, diet, stress reduction, immunization, hygiene, and avoidance of hazardous chemicals and drugs; however, we must also recognize that illness often occurs in spite of all our conscientious efforts to prevent it.

Caring for the sick is not a pleasant or popular task. In cultures where Eastern medicine predominates, the sick are often ignored and left on the streets to die. In contrast, Jesus saw his ministry as one of healing the sick (Mt 9:12; Lk 4:18), and he commissioned his followers to do likewise (Lk 9:1-2; 10:9). As Christians, we must be careful that our desire for wellness does not divert us from ministering to those who are suffering from the ravages of illness.

The techniques of other cultural healing systems adopted by the holistic health movement include acupressure, autogenic exercise, polarity therapy, postural integration, reflexology, various forms of massage and dance, hydrotherapy, therapeutic touch, yoga, psychosynthesis, shamanism, visualization, meditation, T'ai Chi, spiritual healing, relaxation response, herbology and nutrition.[10] Most of these techniques have their roots in Eastern religion and occultism. They may not be spiritually neutral exercises as many holistic practitioners claim. Nursing assessment by some practitioners may include such methods as astrology, numerology (using a person's name and birthdate to reveal aspects of personality), tarot (using a special deck of cards to reveal the inner life of a person), chiromancy (palm reading), graphology (handwriting analysis) and other forms of psychic reading. Blattner, in *Holistic Nursing,* states, "Psychic reading is a *major component* of holistic assessment for those who desire it."[11] The Scriptures forbid us to become involved with occult practices (Lev 19:31; Deut 18:9-14). Even if some occult practices appear to be effective, we cannot justify their use (see Acts 8:9-24). To do so is to deny the lordship of Christ in our lives.

Kenneth Pelletier, a leading spokesman for holistic health, states: "Holistic approaches lead . . . to a whole array of new possibilities for the individual. . . . [The] fundamental reorientation of life style and personal philosophy is the greater issue, of which stress alleviation and the prevention of pathology is but one aspect."[12] The holistic health movement's approach to the general public is experiential, not conceptual. After people have experienced the techniques of holistic health, they are much more likely to become open to the metaphysical assumptions behind them.

The holistic health movement is syncretistic. Advocates are able to incorporate the terminology and tenets of many religions and philosophies into their concepts of health and healing. It is not unusual for holistic healers to quote Jesus or other verses of Scripture, or to claim to be Christians, but they acknowledge neither the uniqueness of Jesus as the Son of God nor the gospel's exclusive claim to truth.[13]

Chow's reference to a "theoretical basis of energy systems, acknowledging the premise of an existing universal, vital life force," is a seemingly unlikely merging of Einstein's theory of relativity and the ancient monistic motto, "All is One." It is both an attempt to lend credence to her theoretical position through use of scientific terminology and a blatantly religious statement. In Eastern and occult religions God is viewed as a universal life force which unites all things. If "All is One" and "One is All," then all is God and God is all. In other words, the self is God.[14] This is different from the Christian view of reality. If everything (and everyone) is an "energy system," and that energy can be redirected at will, then the material world is all an illusion. Pain, suffering and disease are not physically real; they are a state of mind which can be changed through mind control and redistribution of "energy." Blattner states, "Some people can heal through meditation or prayer; for others, it is an act of imagining or visualizing a person as well and whole. Psychic healing is characterized by a spirit of humility and by a *feeling of unity with all other beings.*"[15]

Another characteristic of the holistic health movement is its multidisciplinary team approach. The health care team is expanded to include "all care seen by clients as helpful in maintaining or recovering health, regardless of personal or professional opinions."[16] Chiropractors, spiritualists, traditional ethnic healers and many other types of practitioners not usually accepted by the medical profession are given equal authority with the physician. This egalitarian view of the members of the health team is particularly attractive to nurses, but it puts tremendous responsibility on the client who is forced to coordinate his or her own care and decide which approaches to therapy are best.

Self-responsibility is also a continuous theme in holistic health. Blattner states, "People are responsible for their own bodies and minds. They can choose sickness or health. They have control over their lives and minds, their bodies, and their health." To some extent we can control our attitudes and approach to life, but it is rather overwhelming to hold an individual responsible for all personal illness or injury. A self-responsible person, according to Blattner, does not need the approval of others, has no desire for justice or fairness, sets up his or her own rules of conduct, has eliminated all dependency relationships, never feels guilty and is treated by others the way he or she wants to be treated.[17] To a great extent, this "self-responsible person" resembles a sociopathic personality.

Even the nutritional aspects of holistic health may carry metaphysical overtones. Some practitioners advocate eating foods which balance the *yin* and *yang* to maintain a continuous flow of *chi*. There is a strong emphasis on natural foods, such as whole grains and legumes, which is also being advocated more and more by nutritionists in general. Although the treatment of illness with drugs is often questioned by holistic practitioners, they may enthusiastically prescribe large quantities of vitamin pills.

At first glance, holistic health looks like a refreshing trend which considers the client as a whole person and recognizes the validity of the spiritual dimension of nursing. But it is a different kind of wholeness and a totally different understanding of spirituality from those taught by Christianity. It blurs the distinction between Creator and creature into an all-encompassing "All is One." It views the material world as illusion, and reality as the vital life force of the universe. It is not a logical system, nor is it intended to be. While holistic health practitioners may wholeheartedly incorporate Christian language and practices into their methods of functioning, the Christian cannot be equally open to holistic health. The metaphysical assumptions of holistic health are incompatible with Christian faith.

Wholistic Health in a Christian Context

Wholeness is a biblical concept. Jesus came as the Prince of Peace, the King of Shalom. *Shalom* is the Hebrew word for total well-being, the total restoration of the true state of humanity.[18] The ministry of Jesus was to establish shalom in the world. He taught, he preached, he healed, and he demonstrated the power and love of God in his daily life. His ultimate act to bring us shalom was his actual suffering and death on the cross for our sins. This was no illusion—his suffering and death were real, painful and ugly.

We live in a time when that shalom is already present to some degree, but not yet entirely fulfilled. Romans 8:22-23 tells us, "We know that the whole creation has been groaning in travail together until now; and not only the creation, but we ourselves, who have the first fruits of the Spirit, groan inwardly as we wait for adoption as sons, the redemption of our bodies." In the meantime we are called to enter into the groaning of humanity by feeding the hungry, caring for the sick, clothing the naked, welcoming the stranger and visiting those in prison (Mt 25). The Christian community is the context in which healing and wholeness can legitimately be found; therefore we cannot abandon whole-person health care to practitioners who have an Eastern world view.

Numerous examples of Christian concern for whole-person health care are evident, both historically and in the present. Most of the hospitals in this country were started by Christian groups. Spiritual care was an integral part of the care given by nursing nuns, deaconesses and other Christian nurses. Today, a renewed concern for the spiritual dimension of health care is being revived by groups such as the Wholistic Health Centers, Incorporated, founded by the Rev. Granger Westberg, a Lutheran pastor. Centers are located in church buildings. Clients are cared for by a team of physicians, nurses, clergy and other professionals as needed. The St. Luke Health Centers, Incorporated, of Baltimore also work through church-based health centers. They have an additional emphasis on congregational involvement in healing and health care through prayer and education. Nurses Christian Fellowship has been teaching the principles and practice of spiritual care through workshops, conferences and written materials since its beginning in 1936. The Christian Medical Society assists physicians in integrating their faith with medical practice.

Practicing in a Pluralistic System

We live in an age which is becoming increasingly pluralistic. Until fairly recently almost all health care in America was based on a Judeo-Christian philosophy. Today we function in a health care system which draws upon both Eastern and Western philosophies. Nurses need to be aware of the theological and philosophical understandings behind the modalities of health care being practiced. We also need to be clear about our own beliefs in order to sift through the assortment of ideas and practices which bombard us.

Unfortunately, we do not face an easy task. In many situations the implications of various nursing techniques may seem spiritually loaded, when in actuality they are neutral procedures which have been expressed in spiritual terms. Other times, an approach may be clothed in scientific language, but is in fact an occult practice. Terminology is often confusing and can be used interchangeably. *Holistic* is a term usually used by advocates of Eastern and occult approaches, but not always. Most groups with a Christian perspective who are concerned about whole-person health care use the term *wholistic,* but, again, not always.

Jesus admonished his disciples to be "wise as serpents and innocent as doves" (Mt 10:16). As Christians practicing in a pluralistic health care system, we need to heed his advice. Every new technique must be carefully evaluated, not only for its effectiveness, but also for its philosophical underpinnings. At the same time, we can trust God to guide and protect us from being unknowingly led astray. Some Christians believe that they can use certain holistic health techniques by adapting them to a Christian understanding of their effectiveness. Others adamantly shun all practices which even suggest that their roots may be Eastern or occult. At times we may need to humbly agree to disagree when strong differences of opinion occur among Christians regarding holistic health techniques. The danger of alienating a brother or sister is probably more serious than the risk of compromising our theological understandings. However, we are still responsible before God to be both wise and faithful.

5
Evaluating Holistic Health Modalities
Arlene Miller and Arlynne Ostlund

The following guidelines for evaluating holistic health modalities provide us with a systematic way of assessing the potential religious and philosophical problems hiding behind holistic techniques.

Modality
1. What techniques are necessary to practice the modality (e.g., meditation, "centering," mind control, etc.)?
2. Are assumptions made regarding (a) human nature or (b) the nature of ultimate reality? If so, are they compatible with Scripture?
3. Are these assumptions clearly evident to all observers, or must

one be involved with the modality to determine what they are?
4. What scientific research has been done to support techniques used?
5. What is the level of intervention (e.g., etiology, symptom relief)?

Practitioner
1. What is the practitioner's world view? Does he or she try to persuade clients to accept this world view?
2. Does the practitioner claim a particular source of power? If so, is it compatible with Scripture?
3. Does the practitioner demonstrate an awareness of possible underlying religious assumptions and their implications (see A2)?

Client
1. Does practicing the modality require a change in lifestyle? Is the change compatible with Scripture?
2. Is there improved health? To what extent? For how long?
3. Are there any short- or long-term adverse side effects (physically, mentally, spiritually)?
4. Does a dependency on the practitioner occur?

Results
1. What is the stated explanation for the results?
2. Is the explanation generally accepted by health professionals, or is it subject to controversy?
3. What are other possible explanations?

To sharpen discernment skills, see James W. Sire's *The Universe Next Door* (Downers Grove, Ill.: InterVarsity Press, 1976).

Section 2
Spiritual Care and the Psychiatric Client

6
What Are Spiritual Needs?
Judith Allen Shelly

Spiritual needs of psychiatric clients are seldom recognized and rarely faced, yet they are often the most clearly felt needs of the client. Even the problem that so many distortions and delusions involving religious content occur among emotionally disturbed people attests to the significance of spiritual needs. Clients tend to distort only those things that are intensely meaningful to them. We are by nature religious creatures—spiritual beings— with an inborn tendency to worship and a basic need to know that we fit into a bigger picture than our own little worlds.

A spiritual need is anything necessary to establish or maintain a dynamic, personal relationship with God. The need for love and relatedness, the need to forgive and be forgiven, the need for meaning and purpose, and the need for hope are all spiritual needs. Although each of these needs is experienced and expressed through interpersonal relationships, the ultimate fulfillment can be found only in God.

The need for love is basic to survival. Babies who do not receive love fail to thrive and often die. Children who are not nurtured in a loving atmosphere cannot learn to trust other people or the world around them.

When a person has not learned to give and receive love, disastrous emotional and spiritual problems can result. A positive self-image cannot exist. Others' attempts to show love and support cannot be received. God is seen as an ogre, or nonexistent, or a fanciful means of escape. Consider Linda, a 23-year-old woman with a history of drug abuse and psychosis, who is showing agitated behavior.

Nurse: Linda, are you okay? [*walks over and sits across from her*] What's wrong?

Linda: [*sitting in chair, crying, holding head in hands*] The voices! They just won't leave me alone.

Nurse: What do the voices say, Linda?

Linda: They tell me how ugly and terrible I am.

Nurse: What do you think about yourself, Linda?

Linda: I think I am ugly, too. I can't even be a lady. I'm sloppy, I don't dress right and I eat like a pig.

Nurse: You know, Linda, I like you. Did you ever think about the fact that God loves you and accepts you just the way you are?

Linda: That's hard to believe. I don't think God is like that. I mean, I believe in God and all that, but I don't think that's how it is.

Nurse: Tell me what you think God is like.

Linda: I saw God once when I tripped out on drugs. He was young, and he gave out drugs to everybody—all they wanted. My junkie kind of looked like him. It was really neat.

Linda did not feel loved, and she could not love herself. Drugs were her way of escaping her world of anxiety and alienation, so God appeared in her imagination as a junkie. Linda needed extensive therapy and medication, but she also had a deep spiritual need for love. Linda is one client whose spiritual needs were recognized, and they are now being met.[1]

The need for forgiveness affects our ability to function optimally in daily life. A person who cannot forgive or accept forgiveness is cut off from love and warm relationships. Yet forgiveness is so contrary to human nature that we must look to God for the power to forgive. Our natural tendency is to prove ourselves right or to get even, rather than to say "I'm sorry." An emotionally ill person often finds the problem compounded beyond all measure. Guilt may be so deeply imbedded in the self-concept that forgiveness seems out of the question.

Donna, 17, was admitted to a forensic psychiatric unit after being judged insane at her trial for murdering her baby. She was single and had lived with several boyfriends after leaving home when her parents divorced three years before. The man she was living with when the incident occurred was not the baby's father. Donna sat staring blankly out a window as she talked with a nurse.

"I just couldn't help myself. My baby kept screaming and nothing would make her stop. My boyfriend said he couldn't take it anymore and he was going to kick us out. I didn't have anyplace to go. So I put my hand over her face and held it real tight until she stopped screaming. I didn't know she was dead! I feel so awful. I deserve to go to hell. I keep praying for God to strike me dead, but I know he doesn't listen to me. I'm too rotten."

Donna had a problem with very real guilt—she had killed her baby—but she also had an underlying struggle with guilt feelings which had been going on since childhood. She felt guilty when her parents fought and assumed that she was responsible for their divorce. She felt guilty about her promiscuity, but she did not know how to stop it. She felt guilty for just being alive, and forgiveness was a foreign concept to her.

As much as our culture talks about the basic goodness of human nature, most people are very aware of their own sinfulness. We wear our guilt like a weight upon our shoulders, and it becomes a persistent barrier to loving and open relationships with other people. It is good news indeed when we read, "If we say we have no sin, we deceive ourselves, and the truth is not in us. If we confess our sins, he is faithful and just, and will forgive our sins and cleanse us from all unrighteousness" (1 Jn 1:8-9).

The need for meaning and purpose is often masked in the hectic lifestyles of active people. Long- and short-term goals distract us from thinking too seriously about the ultimate issues of life. We have children to raise, a career to develop, mortgage payments to make, a new car to buy and a whirlwind of social activities. But illness—either physical or emotional—brings a grinding halt to many temporal pursuits.

Suddenly the human relationships which gave meaning to a person's life may be terminated or badly strained. There may be no career to develop if a person is too ill to hold a job. The financial drain of illness may leave a person unable to strive for any material possessions, and even unable to provide for a family. Stripped of all that gave life meaning and purpose, a person begins to ask, "Why, then, am I here?"

Mike was a 68-year-old retired factory worker. He had been forced to retire at age 62 when his plant laid off a large number of workers. Without a regular job Mike felt useless. He spent most of his time in front of the television with a beer in his hand, or sitting in a bar until closing time.

"Three years ago I was just about dead. I was in a coma for eight days. The doctors said there wasn't anything that could be done for me anymore. The alcohol was killing me. They sent me to a rehabilitation place and I started with AA. I haven't had a drink since. But I'm still an alcoholic. I'm just one drink away all the time," Mike related to the nurse.

"It sounds like you are afraid you might take another drink sometime."

"I can't think of anything that would make me do that again.

I've been through everything. I don't know of anything that would make me drink again. God gave me a new life, and he keeps me from drinking."

Part of Mike's new life was speaking at Alcoholics Anonymous meetings around the area and counseling other alcoholics. He began to find meaning in his life because he could help other people. He knew his life was a gift from God and he wanted to live it accordingly.[2]

According to an ancient proverb, the lack of hope can precipitate mental illness. Proverbs 13:12 tells us, "Hope deferred makes the heart sick." Hope is a spiritual need because realistic hope must be based on the knowledge that a loving, personal God is in control of the world and involved in my life.

Marvin was an 80-year-old man with chronic organic brain disease. He had no living relatives. In the rare times that he was lucid he would become depressed about being in a state hospital with so many "frightening people." Marvin had no hope for recovery or for being released from the hospital, but Marvin had hope. He looked forward to going to heaven to be with Jesus and his wife. In the meantime Marvin would sing hymns and pray. Even when he was unable to carry on a rational conversation, he could recite the Twenty-third Psalm and pray the Lord's Prayer. He knew all the verses to "What a Friend We Have in Jesus," and he sang them loudly and clearly over and over again.

Spiritual Needs in a Psychiatric Setting

If spiritual needs are so important and so obvious, why are they so seldom recognized and met? Spiritual needs in a psychiatric setting present a special set of problems which may hinder proper assessment and intervention.

First, we are faced with the problem of distortions. Not all expressions of spirituality are healthy. In many cases, a person's unhealthy religious beliefs contribute to illness and impede progress in therapy. Religious delusions may cause nurses to respond to the content of the delusion rather than to the underlying spiritual need. Sociopathic and borderline personalities may use religion as a manipulative technique. When a person is mentally ill, all aspects of thinking and feeling can be distorted and confused. Religion is no exception. A person with a poor self-concept and unsatisfactory interpersonal relationships will usually have a distorted concept of God and a broken relationship with him.

Another problem we face in recognizing spiritual needs of psychiatric clients is that religious language is often abstract and symbolic. A person who is able to think only concretely will easily misinterpret theological concepts, Bible passages and religious symbols. Whenever a client talks about religious ideas and spiritual concepts we must be very careful to determine if what we hear is what is meant. If a client tells you that God is her father, she may mean it quite literally—and also think that she is Jesus.

Finally, the very intensity of spiritual needs in emotionally ill persons may prevent us from recognizing them. People may be so cut off from human love that they cannot even conceive of a loving God. Clients may be so consumed by neurotic guilt that the real meaning of sin and forgiveness is beyond their understanding. Life may seem so void of meaning and purpose that the hope of a relationship with a personal God may seem like nothing but "pie in the sky." In many cases, clients may need extensive counseling and therapy before they are able to work on their spiritual needs.

In the following chapters, we will examine the basic spiritual needs and how they are expressed by psychiatric clients. Then we will take a closer look at the problems which hinder assessment and intervention. Spiritual needs are important. Responsible nursing care must include the spiritual dimension if our goal is to help the client find optimal mental health.

7
Healthy and Unhealthy Religious Beliefs
Sandra D. John

Most Christians, at least initially, tend to think that all talk about God is healthy and an open door to share their own faith. Many non-Christian therapists believe that all talk about God and religious ideation is pathological and to be avoided. Both extremes result from a lack of understanding and experience, and both can create problems in therapy. Wayne Oates, a pastoral counselor and professor of psychiatry, suggests that the use of religious language by patients can provide a "royal road" to the deeper level of problems the person is trying to solve.[1] To avoid patients' religious concerns can cut off a valuable means of therapy. However, the religious language of a severely disturbed individual can mean something entirely different to the patient than to the therapist. It is essential to uncover what the patient means by what he says about God, the Bible and other religious ideas. Not all religious beliefs are healthy, and many therapists have encountered Christian beliefs only in their distorted form in patients, so they are understandably leery of religious talk.

Just as mental health is a difficult term to define, spiritual or religious health is hard to pin down. Spiritual health is also a "dynamic equilibrium" and a "vital balance." It is seldom static. The concept of a healthy or unhealthy spiritual life is an extremely difficult, but essential, discrimination to make. It can best be measured on a series of continua, rather than with a checklist of symptoms. In general, a healthy religion joins the whole person with God, self, others and the environment in the past, present and future.

The thrust toward wholeness is central to a healthy religion, whereas an unhealthy religion separates and fragments the person. Wayne Oates states:

> A healthy faith is the expression of the total personality of an individual in his relationship to the Divine as his ultimate and comprehensive loyalty. When . . . religion becomes either a segregated, autonomous system in an airtight compartment separated from the rest of life, or it becomes a disturbing factor in the total functioning of the person, . . . it is sick.[2]

Gordon Allport distinguishes between mature and immature religion by noting the following tensions: (1) self-expansion vs. wish-fulfillment and self-gratification, (2) self-objectification with detachment and insight vs. lack of reflection and inability to judge the self and (3) integration and self-unification vs. fragmentary, spasmodic and segmented thinking. "A mature religious sentiment," he states, "seems never satisfied unless it is dealing with matters central to all existence."[3] Six continua provide further insights into the health or maturity of a person's faith.

Sin and Guilt

The first continuum gauges a sense of sin and guilt. The healthy middle view recognizes that I have separated myself from God by choices I have made, and that I am both ultimately restored to God through the person and work of Jesus Christ and daily experiencing forgiveness and restoration. The unhealthy ends of the continuum are, on the one hand, preoccupation with the unpardonable sin, inability to accept forgiveness, and belief that one is totally without hope and redemption. The other end of the spectrum is the absence of a sense of sin and the lack of values and standards of right and wrong. A person at this extreme has no guilt feelings.

Theologian J. I. Packer summarizes the two extremes of dealing with guilt by saying, "There are two sorts of sick consciences, those that are not aware enough of sin and those that are not aware enough of pardon."[4] Assessing a person's awareness of sin, both its strength and the issues that trigger it, is extremely sensitive and requires a finely tuned spiritual awareness, one which a nurse and client will be continually struggling to develop.

Focus on sinfulness without forgiveness may be manifested in a variety of ways. One is an obsessive fear of making mistakes. A person this fearful can make no decisions. Another is a concept of the self as totally sinful, worthless and wretched.

Larry, for example, was so obsessed with his inability to control what he felt was excessive sexual fantasizing that he felt the only way he could relate to God was on the basis of asking forgiveness for his sin. He believed he might be the antichrist because of such a terrible sin, yet he could not conceive of what his life would be without it.

Donald continually paced back and forth, rubbing his hands together and repeating, "I'm hopeless. God can't forgive me. I ought to be dead."

Gail constantly felt guilty for being alive. She had been sexually abused as a child and somehow felt she had deserved it. She felt responsible for the death of her twin at birth and also for her parents' divorce when she was thirteen.

A person's tone may reveal a view of God as judgmental, harsh and condemning rather than forgiving, even when the person is verbally accepting love and forgiveness. Tony, for example, spoke of God's love and wanting to "glorify" him, but he did so in a harsh and angry tone of voice and with a strained facial expression.

On the other hand, the person who has no moral values or standards is also unbalanced. This person may experience God as a Santa Claus and see the universe revolving around himself. Persons traditionally labeled sociopaths might fit at this end of the continuum. For instance, Arthur was addicted to heroine and killed a shopkeeper while stealing to support his habit. "He was in my way," Arthur told the nurse without emotion.

Often the lack of guilt feelings is subtly expressed. Periods of profuse "repentance" may be used to manipulate helping persons. Marcia was a good example. She was recently released from a state hospital. Several Christian nurses, who had developed a therapeutic relationship with Marcia during their psychiatric experience as students, invited her to live with them. Marcia very quickly made life difficult for her roommates with her manipulative behavior. Whenever she was directly confronted she would take an overdose of tranquilizers. Finally the nurses asked Marcia to move out.

The next day Marcia came home and announced that she wanted to receive Christ. Tearfully, she told her roommates that their witness had convinced her to become a Christian. After one month of radically changed behavior, Marcia resumed her old patterns. Her roommates asked her to move again. Marcia moved in with friends of her former roommates. Two weeks later one of Marcia's new roommates told her friends that Marcia had become a Christian the day before. The cycle was repeated each time Marcia's security was threatened. She "became a Christian" six times, for six sets of people, before she moved to another town and severed contact with her former roommates.

Freedom and Restraint
Healthy individuals live with a mixture of creativity, spontaneity and discipline. They are able to experience the freedom and joy

of living with a full range of emotional expression. Sexuality and aggression are used for constructive and responsible enhancement of life. They can tolerate ambiguity and appreciate humor. They can freely express honest feelings to God.

The two contrasting ends of the continuum emphasize either too much freedom (having no rules, constraints or limitations), or a compulsive lack of freedom. Having no rules is similar to feeling no sense of sin and is characterized by licentiousness and lack of responsibility for the consequences of personal actions. Pam represented one end of the continuum. While deciding whether or not to commit suicide, she told a nurse, "It's my life, isn't it? Don't I have a right to do with it what I please?"

The other end of the continuum is manifested as legalism, authoritarianism, a feeling of being driven or of having no enjoyment, repressing sexuality and emotions, and emphasizing obedience only out of fear rather than joy. Such persons can never do enough to please themselves or God. They live in bondage to doing more and working harder.

Betty demonstrated such behavior. She felt guilty if she wasn't working constantly, and she apologized to everyone if she wasn't busy. She spent ten minutes drying each glass when she did dishes, and she was constantly cleaning. She was overloaded with church work but felt she couldn't turn down a volunteer job or she would appear selfish. She apologized for mistrusting her brother-in-law who helped her with finances after her husband's death. "I'm not supposed to say anything negative about him if I'm a good Christian," she said.

God's Control

A third continuum outlines a person's view of the level of God's activity in human affairs. A healthy person walks a delicate balance: he knows there is a Supreme Being who is ultimately in control of the universe and upon whom we finite humans are wholly dependent, while at the same time he realizes that this God has given us human responsibility and the ability to make choices.

Philippians 2:12-13 spells out both dimensions of this: "Work out your own salvation with fear and trembling; for God is at work in you, both to will and to work for his good pleasure."

Oates, borrowing from Jan Ehrenwald, describes this balance as the capacity to shift between the two existential modalities of the sacred and the profane, the prayer and the personal effort. This balance integrates the "empirical-pragmatic world of causal relations and the persuasive-ideological world of convincing values."[5]

Foundational to the ability to walk this balance is a basic trust in the universe and God's goodness. Such trust engenders a realistic, well-founded hope upon which one can then make daily practical decisions. This may be contrasted with the sick hopes outlined by Erikson: (1) delusions which are not founded in reality, (2) addictions that are intense but not lasting and (3) depressions without hope at all.[6]

One unhealthy view sees God as intervening directly in every minute human decision. This view expects special revelation without any human mediation. For example, Polly was unable to make even the smallest decision for herself such as getting up, getting dressed or brushing her teeth unless "God tells me to." Thus her life was completely incapacitated.

Closely connected with such a view of God's direct intervention in human affairs is a "magical" view of God's activity. For example, Rosa finally admitted her alcoholism verbally but refused to attend Alcoholics Anonymous or to accept any other human assistance. She said, "I've made up my mind that I won't drink again, and all I need to do is pray."

In another situation, when a nurse commented to Judy how nice it had been to have steak for dinner, she replied, "I know. I asked God for it." Judy believed the Bible was able to do special things for her, so she carried it with her everywhere and had it occupy a chair of its own beside her.

Ecstatic religious experience may also be used as a magical interpretation of God's activity. Jeff realized in counseling that he needed a "high" in his life which he had been finding in alcohol, drugs and sex. After joining a charismatic group, he decided he could become "high on Jesus," but he was unable to apply his faith to daily life.

A magical view of God can also take a fatalistic form. Andy stated, "I don't need to make any plans for my future. Whatever happens, God will fix it up for me."

The other end of the continuum reveals a grandiose view of humanity, a belief that we can act entirely on our own and do not need God. Oates classifies this unhealthy form of religious belief as a kind of idolatry, "absolutizing the finite."[7] This can take the form of basic doubt in the universe, manifested by an excessive need to control everything and everybody, or it can be seen in the belief that God left the universe to capriciousness, is not involved in daily life, and is not available to us. Nancy says, "When I need people they aren't there. I believe God won't be there for me when I need him either."

Self-Estimate

Self-esteem is central to any definition of mental health. A healthy religious life strengthens one's view of self without causing self-centeredness or boasting. To know and experience that I am created, loved unconditionally and redeemed by God gives me a deep sense of my own worth and value. It allows me to accept myself deeply with humility, to live openly and vulnerably, to be congruous inside and out, and to accept the limitations of finitude. With strengthened self-esteem I am able to reach past myself and be motivated by concern for others, not by self-fear and wish-fulfillment.

The two unhealthy edges of the continuum are a very poor self-esteem on one end and grandiosity on the other. A poor self-estimate may be demonstrated by a person who finds identity from another rather than from within. Susan is a schizophrenic teen who nods her head constantly in imitation of a nurse listening to another patient. Janet considered suicide when rejected by her boyfriend, because she had allowed him to determine the worth of her life. "Worm" theology—belief in "a God who really deep down underneath consider[s] me to be less than dirt"[8]—is another example of an unhealthy self-estimate. Paula articulated, "I just feel that I wasn't supposed to be born or be alive somehow."

Poor self-esteem, like a lack of freedom or trust, may be manifested behaviorally by constant work. The person may try to earn personal worth and God's favor by effort.

The other side of this continuum may be seen most extremely in the person who claims to be God, Jesus, a saint or a biblical character. A less extreme example would be anyone who says, "I can make it on my own without God." The basic characteristic of this end of the continuum is the inability to recognize finitude and dependency. Bruce believed God had sent him with a special mission, that he was a prophet to foretell the end of the world and that God spoke to him directly through a halo on his head. Cathy had delusions of being able to read minds and dwell in the "astrophysical realm and entirely in the spirit." She said, "I don't want to be an ordinary person or be in a body. It's too hard to live an ordinary life."

Concept of Suffering

A healthy person accepts suffering and persecution as part of the human condition and draws on God's strength to face it realistically rather than trying to escape it. A healthy person can grow through suffering and find a deepening relationship with God.

One unhealthy end of this continuum is demonstrated by Fred, who believed his emotional illness meant that he was not claiming God's promises sufficiently. He had been told that if he really concentrated on the Bible, he would never experience anything but prosperity. To him this meant no physical or emotional illness and plenty of material resources. He refused to take his medication because to do so would not indicate reliance on God, his source of prosperity.

A related unhealthy view is that all suffering or death must be punishment, because one who has not committed a sin has no struggles or problems—emotional, physical or material. A more healthy perspective is that there usually is no direct link between suffering and punishment, although the consequences of behavior exist even after forgiveness. Trish promised to pray one hour a day, which she found impossible to do. She then felt that God was "breaking" her for her failure.

At the opposite end of the continuum is the view that Christians should expect and even welcome suffering. Tim constantly intruded into the lives of others, feeling a compulsion to tell everyone about Jesus. "I'm sure they will reject me, but I'm supposed to suffer for the name of Jesus." He often prayed all night, forcing himself to go without sleep to be "a martyr for the Lord and my friends." Cindy received much secondary gain from being depressed and feeling self-pity. "Well, it's a Christian's lot in life," she said with a sigh.

As with all the continua, discriminating between health and illness can be extremely sensitive. Spiritual sacrifice and asceticism may be healthy in a person's total life, or it may become self-destructive or punitive. A day of fasting and prayer is likely to enhance a person's relationship with God, whereas anorexia nervosa is unlikely to do so. The entire context of the person's life and history must be considered.

Relationships
Finally, a healthy religious belief builds bridges, not barriers, between people and fosters interdependence with others. The healthy person has an individual self-identity which leads to the formation of supportive, mutual relationships with others.

Unhealthy beliefs drastically separate an individual from others, or a group of people from the mainstream of society or religious thought. Social isolation, a need to withdraw from the rest of the world, and private individualistic beliefs contrast with the community focus of the whole of Scripture. Jack wanted to avoid people on the unit and spend all his time alone in his room reading his

Bible. Ginny was afraid to be vulnerable to others for fear of losing her independence, so she had no close friendships. Paul was so concerned about those who held different beliefs from his own that he became a religious witch-hunter. He focused on differences rather than similarities and had an "us against them" mentality. Al thought he was to use God's Word as a weapon. He used to be violent with his fists, "but now I want to scare people with words."

People at the other extreme may have no personal identity or be totally absorbed into a group identity. Others outwardly exhibit extreme independence while inwardly feeling total dependence or enmeshment. Kathleen felt she had no meaning in life apart from a relationship with a man. Her Christian community, which gave little role identity to the single woman, reinforced her feeling. David understood Scripture to teach that one must give oneself over to God so totally as to exclude all personal opinions. David did not assert himself and could not take any compliments. Georgia belonged to a cult which told her exactly what to do each moment. She made no personal decisions and found her identity totally as a member of the group. When the group disbanded after a leadership crisis, Georgia was immobilized and unable to function.

The use of religious authority to manipulate others is another aspect of the unhealthy end of the continuum. Both the person who is authoritarian and the one who allows another person to control his or her life are less than fully self-integrative.

Religion is healthy when it moves an individual or system toward wholeness and integration. It becomes sick when it moves toward fragmentation. A healthy person finds a middle balancing point in each continuum described. Self-reflection, humility and sensitivity are essential when assessing an individual or system. Each of us fluctuates in our own positions on the continua. We can only stand with clients with unhealthy religious beliefs, gently nudging them toward balance in a precarious world.

HEALTHY AND UNHEALTHY RELIGIOUS BELIEFS
THE CONTINUA

Sense of Sin and Guilt
Absense of sense of
right and wrong

Forgiven sinner, able to forgive others,
balance of God's lovingkindness and judgment

No acceptance
of forgiveness

Freedom and Restraint
No restraints

Creativity, freedom, and spontaneity with
discipline

Compulsive lack of
freedom

God's Activity in Human Affairs
All human activity, no God

Human responsibility within God's sovereignty,
balance of God's transcendence and immanence

Magical view of God's
direct interventions, no human
responsibility

Self-Estimate
Grandiosity, hubris, no recognition of
finitude

Created by God, unique, valuable, loved,
worthwhile, gifted

Self-hatred, rejection,
destruction

Concept of Suffering
No physical, material or mental want

Can bring good out of suffering, can endure it
with strength, but does not seek it

Glorify and seek suffering

Relationship with Others
No personal identity, enmeshed with
others, overly dependent

Community, bridge with others, individual identity
with interdependence

Segregation, barrier with
others, "lone ranger," overly
independent

8
Assessing Spiritual Needs
Sandra D. John

Margaret looked at me with a flat affect and said, "I don't feel there is any meaning to life if I'm not needed by anyone. The people who used to need me have rejected me now. I'm not sure God loves me, either." For months Margaret had been becoming more and more disorganized, forgetful and unable to think clearly. She had stopped going out of the house. She spent most of her time sitting around the house in her bathrobe. She was a widow and lived alone. Last week her daughter did not return her phone call, and her depression became unbearable. This was her first counseling session.

Does Margaret have a spiritual need? The first step in the nursing process is a thorough assessment. In a psychiatric setting, assessment is intervention to some extent. Truly understanding what the hurting person is trying to communicate is the beginning of meeting the expressed needs. A thorough psychosocial assessment, developmental level assessment, psychiatric history and mental status examination are requisites in the assessment process. It is also important to assess the function of spirituality in the person's life—to evaluate what the person is trying to communicate by religious language and what the person is expressing behind religious symbolism. In assessing the client's use of religious symbols and ideation, the nurse is asking, What do the symbols and ideation mean for this person in the light of her past history, in the context of her immediate stress, and for her future hope and ongoing spiritual integrity?

First, a thorough history of a person's religious interest, feelings, thoughts and behavior is necessary. These important questions must be asked:

1. How did the religious interest arise? Gradually or suddenly?
2. How does the religious ideation relate to the person's background, family, culture and subculture? Is the person conforming to or rebelling against a religious upbringing?
3. How was the person first introduced to religious ideas?
4. What is the relationship between the development of the mental illness and the religious concern? Which arose first?
5. At what developmental level is the person's religious understanding and behavior operating?

Margaret, who was raised in a Christian home, was interested in religious things from childhood, but her background was legalistic and stressed external motivation. She was more concerned about what others thought than she was with her own motivation and responses. Now at age 65 she is rebelling against her religious upbringing, causing extreme spiritual and psychological struggles within herself.

Margaret's family used religion to control her and restrict her behavior. This caused her to view God as a critical parent and in turn to use religion to control her own daughter. She hated the way her mother used religion for social status, control and conformity. She resented the approval her sister received for conforming while she was rejected for rebelling. She dislikes seeing the same patterns developing in her relationship with her daughter, and she wants to change.

Margaret's mental illness and religious concern arose together. The unhealthy religion of her childhood contributed to her lack of self-acceptance, her manipulative use of religion with others, her feelings of restraint rather than a free choice of beliefs, and the unhealthy dependence and enmeshment with her mother which spilled over into her relationship with her own daughter. At age 65 she is in an adolescent stage of religious development, seeking to find her own religious identity. At this stage she is also recapitulating earlier tasks of autonomy versus shame and doubt and of establishing independence from her mother.

Cynthia was a 25-year-old woman with an entirely different religious experience from Margaret's, but it also entered into her mental illness. Cynthia's chief presenting symptoms were depression, suicidal threats, anxiety, sleeping only four to five hours a night with early morning awakening, erratic eating habits, inability to hold a job and an increase in alcohol consumption. Her religious interest arose suddenly. She was raised in a nonpracticing Roman Catholic home and attended Catholic high school, but did not become interested in religion until moving to the West Coast last year and living with an aunt and uncle who were evangelical Christians. This was the first time she had ever been away from her family.

One night soon after she arrived she woke up having an urge to read the Bible and pray, which she then did for several hours each night for a week. Her aunt and uncle were away, but she talked to a neighbor who "prayed with me to have a personal relationship with Jesus Christ." She subsequently became involved with a conservative, legalistic local church.

Cynthia's mental illness arose before her religious interest. Three years ago, while she was a student, she had a psychotic break at a time when she was experiencing difficulty in school, a broken relationship with a man and anxiety over her sister's divorce. She was in psychotherapy and on antipsychotic medication from that time until moving west. She stopped taking her medication three months before coming to the community mental health clinic. I believe Cynthia had an authentic religious experience which grew out of a need for reorganization, structure and security in her life. Developmentally, she was at a basic level of learning to trust God and herself in her first experience of real independence.

Functions of Religious Behavior and Ideation

According to some conceptualizations of the meaning of feelings, thoughts and behavior in mental and emotional illness, the primary drive is to decrease anxiety. Religious behavior and ideation may serve this function by returning a person to a more secure period of existence or by organizing and ritualizing life. It may offer strength from within and beyond oneself to deal with the present crisis.

Sometimes it is best to build up religious defenses, thus decreasing anxiety. At other times the nurse should help decrease defenses in order to increase the anxiety required to facilitate needed life changes. Religious content may be used to do either.

After a superficial suicide attempt, Brian told a nurse he wanted to believe that if he committed suicide he would go to hell. This frightened him enough, he explained, to deter him from doing what he did not really want to do. In this situation, the staff chose to encourage his religious belief as a means of impulse control.

After a broken relationship with a girlfriend, Karl became suicidal and was admitted to the hospital. His ego boundaries were somewhat tenuous, but he was oriented, had connected thought processes and was open to using the hospital to make some major life decisions. Karl was in conflict about his sexual and personal behavior and his identity as a Christian. The team plan was to help him examine the reasons for and consequences of his choices rather than to tell him what to do. We encouraged him to explore his religious convictions and behavior on his own; then we supported him in dealing with the tension his choices created.

The religious content in mental illness may also be an attempt to communicate deep needs of feelings about oneself and one's situation. The goal of any communication exchange with a psychiatric client is to understand what the person is feeling and trying to share of himself. This is doubly true for spiritual needs. Spiritual needs include love and relatedness, forgiveness, meaning and purpose, and hope.

During Paul's acutely psychotic state he spoke constantly of astroprojection and of being in a "spiritual body," not a physical one. After he recompensated, he stated plainly that his life was so uncomfortable, with so little hope, that such thinking gave him a way to escape his intolerable existence. He also focused a great deal on "the Second Coming of the Lord." He described with gusto being one of the "righteous" who would go to heaven, while the "unrighteous" would be tortured. This earthly life, he explained, was so unsatisfying to him that the only hope he could envision was the idea of a heavenly existence which others would not share.

Levels of Religious Concern

Pastoral counselor Wayne Oates describes five levels of religious concern. Understanding these levels can be helpful in assessing the spiritual needs of clients.[1]

Superficial religious concern is seen in the person who had no substantial concern about spirituality before the onset of mental illness. Present concern is more apparent than real. The person is engaging in "plank-grabbing" behavior as he or she decompensates, or the person may be using religion to avoid responsibility or to gain attention.

Peter showed superficial religious concern. He had shown no previous religious interest, but when his wife filed for divorce he began to experience deep emotional ups and downs. He began to categorize everything and everyone as "good" or "bad." He suddenly identified himself as "good and for God," while his wife and her friends were "bad and against God." When his acute upset passed, he no longer had any concern about God.

Carol had been raised in a Roman Catholic family. She had visited other churches, but with no serious interest. Hospitalized for chronic self-destructive ideation and behavior in a severe personality disorder, she desperately sought time and attention from everyone. When the nurses set firm limits, insisting that she speak only with her assigned staff person, she requested a visit from the chaplain. She asked to speak to on-call chaplains when the regular chaplain was off duty, even though she had regular appointments with the assigned chaplain. When she wanted to see the chaplain at an unscheduled time and was reminded of their next appointment, she yelled, "I'll commit suicide . . . and I don't know if I believe in God . . . and even the chaplain won't talk to me!"

Conventional religious concern is seen in the person who may have attended church as a social conventionality or because of family tradition, but whose religious concern is not personal, meaningful or truly helpful. This person may name a religious preference on admission and then never mention religion again, or may talk in a casual manner about some behavior, ritual or teaching from childhood religious education. He or she is not likely to focus on spirituality as an issue, or to consider how it might be personally meaningful or integrated into all of life. The conventionally religious person is unlikely to consider the relationship between spirituality and the present psychosocial dilemma; however, religious behavior and gatherings may serve a valuable social function.

Ruth gave her religious affiliation as "Protestant" on the hospital admission form. Admitted for chronic depression, she avoided most group activities in the ward, but she always participated when someone began a hymn sing. She told the nurse that she enjoyed being part of a group having fun. When the nurse suggested that she might also enjoy the ward prayer group, Ruth recoiled. "Those people are too religious," she said. "They make me nervous!"

Compulsive religious concern is a ritualistic, forced religious expression seen in obsessive-compulsive kinds of behavior. It is often seen in persons with a long history of unhealthy religious training or with a superimposed depression.

Anna was diagnosed with involutional melancholia in an obsessive-compulsive personality style. Her life became almost unmanageable with all her compulsive rituals to arrange her room, food items on her tray and personal hygiene. She performed certain prayer rituals at specific times of the day and became acutely upset if they were disturbed. Her strict rules of behavior centered especially on sexual and cleanliness issues and seemed to increase when she was anxious.

Randy, raised in the Roman Catholic tradition, found his relationship with God sustaining and comforting in the loss of a good friend. At the same time, he exhibited some compulsive religious concern in his sexuality. He was frustrated that, as a single man, he was unable to release his sexual feelings, and expressed anger at God for making rigid rules for sexual expression. He began to swear at God and have obsessive thoughts about sexual intercourse with the Virgin Mary. He would then quickly retract these thoughts, substituting phrases which he compulsively repeated for repentance.

Religious concern in character disorders is a use of religion to seduce or abuse others. People who use religion this way are ordinarily not seen in psychiatric-mental health settings, but they may come to the dramatic attention of the public when exposed by the news media. Some cult leaders and false evangelists fall in this category. Sometimes drug and alcohol abusers will profess religious faith in order to avoid imprisonment or other consequences of their behavior. Persons with borderline personalities are also sometimes encountered in churches, where they can create great upheaval and dissension.

Joanne moved into a new neighborhood, and immediately she and her family joined the local church. One month later she called the pastor and told him that her husband had lost his job and that they did not have enough food for the week. A special offering was collected and groceries were delivered by members of the congregation. The pattern was repeated several times before it was discovered that the husband was working as well as collecting unemployment and welfare payments. Joanne was also appealing to other churches for money, saying that her own church would not help her. When confronted with her behavior Joanne stopped coming to church, but she continued to ask for money occasionally.

Authentic religious concern is evident when the client turns to religion to seek an interpretation of the chaos in his or her life, to find meaning in the situation and to turn in true dependence on God. Anton Boison, a clergyman who has been a psychiatric patient, says that both religion and functional mental illness are attempts to organize one's life around a new center for meaning and purpose.[2]

Barbara, once a churchgoer with conventional religious concern, stated during her psychiatric hospitalization, "I've decided who Jesus really is, and I just want to deeply experience and feel him. I've had people leave me over and over, and I've got to learn that Jesus doesn't leave. I need to find out the meaning of this experience."

The categories of religious concern described by Oates will often be seen in various combinations in the same person. One aspect of a person's faith may be authentic and healthy while another aspect may be unhealthy. A person may also shift from one category to another as general mental health improves or disintegrates. Correctly assessing a client's religious concern will enable a nurse to assist in the movement toward spiritual health.

Correlation of Religious Beliefs with Mental Illness

A client's religious beliefs may have a strong cause-and-effect relationship to his or her mental illness. Mental illness may, in turn, cause religious concern to become distorted and unhelpful. Assessing the cause-and-effect relationships between religious beliefs and mental illness will provide direction in planning nursing care. Healthy religious concern can then be supported, and unhealthy religious ideation can be discussed in therapy. In assessing the correlation between religious beliefs and mental illness, a nurse may consider the following questions.

1. Does the person's religious behavior or input seem to create emotional disturbance or contribute in some way to its development?

Charles, 24, was seeking to find his personal identity. Torn between becoming a minister and an actor, he felt that if he became a minister he should not have any sexual desires or angry thoughts. If he became an actor, on the other hand, he felt that he could not remain a Christian. When he was not sure of who he was, he felt compelled to attempt suicide "like a famous actor." His religious training taught him to consider the sacred good and the secular evil. So much of life had been declared sinful that he could see no way to integrate his thoughts, feelings and career choices with his faith.

2. Is the religious aspect of the person's behavior an indirect precipitating factor in the emotional disorder?

Cathy was afraid of making decisions because she was afraid of making mistakes, and previous decisions had led to traumatic losses. She had lived rather dependently upon her parents until an early marriage. She then became equally dependent upon her husband. The marriage soon ended in divorce, and she was left with little structure in her life. During that time she attended a meeting of a youth cult with her brother. The following weekend she experienced a psychotic break. The disorganization was brief and her continued involvement in the cult structured her life for a while. When she began to have doubts about the group, she became acutely disturbed again. Her primary symptom was extreme ambivalence in decision making. Her personality structure seemed to interplay with the strictly authoritarian group, creating overwhelming conflict and tension.

3. Is the religious concern a symptom of a deeper conflict?

Gerald, 28, was raised in a conservative Protestant home. As a teen he dabbled in Eastern religions. As an adult he switched to Roman Catholicism. Diagnosed as a paranoid schizophrenic since his teens, he was still trying to find his own identity apart from his parents. He would drink and then direct a great deal of hostility at his parents' religious group (which believed in absolute abstinence from alcohol). He would also direct his paranoid thinking toward hospital staff who were of a different religion or nationality, saying he was being persecuted for being Catholic and Italian (which he was not).

4. Is the religious concern a defense that is not healthy long-term, but presently prevents further decompensation?

Gloria was hospitalized for alcoholism after admitting for the first time that she was alcohol-dependent. She was a leader in her church and declared that she did not need help from anyone to stop drinking. She said that God would take away her desire to drink and give her the ability to totally abstain. At this stage in her disease a heavy reliance on God will be strengthening, but she will also need to become involved with a support group and make some internal changes in order to remain sober.

5. Are the religious behavior and thinking realistic, comforting and supportive?

Vivian, 81, was hospitalized for an acute anxiety and depressive reaction following a three-year period during which she suffered the loss of six close relationships. She had a strong personal faith in Jesus and was an active church member. She recognized that the roots of her anxiety and depression were found in events surrounding her son's death. She knew she needed to "let go" of her son and forgive her daughter-in-law who, she felt, had prevented proper medical care for him and had been "mean" to him in the last months of his life. She found comfort, support and direction through prayer, reading the Bible and talking with others about her faith. She communicated her feelings directly to God and found models of feeling expression, prayer and sustenance in Scripture.

6. What part does religion play in the choice of symptoms?

Two studies show some significant correlation between certain religious groups and specific psychiatric diagnoses and choices of symptoms.

A study in Australia, reported in the *British Journal of Psychiatry,* compared total inpatient psychiatric admissions and total population with those admissions giving Jehovah's Witness as their religious preference and Jehovah's Witnesses in the total population. It showed that Jehovah's Witnesses had twice as many psychiatric hospital admissions as the general population, three times as many schizophrenics, and four times as many paranoid schizophrenics.[3] This raises many questions. Do Jehovah's Witnesses attract unstable people? Do people join because of their emotional needs? Does this group promote an unhealthy emotional life and precipitate illness? Is there some correlation, but not necessarily a direct cause-and-effect relationship?

Studies of various religious groups (Jewish, Catholic and several Protestant denominations) showed Jewish persons to have the largest percentage of drinkers, but the smallest percentage of heavy drinkers. Baptist have the smallest percentage of drinkers, but those who do drink have the highest percentage of alcohol-related problems. Jewish religion has a unified cultural control on drunkenness and rituals surrounding the use of alcohol in religious ceremonies. Baptists are likely to associate all drinking with sin and guilt. Alcohol can be used as a form of rebellion in groups which advocate abstinence, but not where drinking in prescribed ways is sanctioned.[4]

7. Does the religion merely provide the content ideation for the illness or delusion? What is the process beyond the content?

Acute psychotic delusions, especially paranoid delusions, may be expressed in religious terminology. Frank was acutely psychotic and yelled almost constantly, vacillating between obscenities and religious phrases. Religious symbols and the language of good and evil spoke for him and the conflict in his own warring feelings.

Larry had difficulty with his ego boundaries, especially in regard to sexuality. He had been raised in a Christian home where the Bible was studied. Now he wondered if "talking with a woman means having sex with her," because he had been told during a Bible study of John 4 that in Christ's time it was considered so.

Harry, 63, felt rejected and abandoned by his family in the hospital. He expressed his feelings with religious symbolism, saying that the devil had him hostage in the hospital.

Laura, 26, had a borderline diagnosis. She harbored extreme rage toward her mother and tended to expect others to fulfill the mother role which her own mother would not. She asked to speak to a hospital chaplain because she wanted to express her anger at God for not doing what she wanted him to do. She expected God to get her a job, an apartment and the custody of her daughter.

The assessment phase of the nursing process is essential for understanding the function of a person's religious thoughts, feelings and behavior, and what the person is trying to communicate through religious language or symbolism. The religious concern can then be viewed from the perspective of a client's entire life history and present context. The depth of a nurse's understanding, and the nurse's ability to communicate this understanding to the client, is the beginning intervention in meeting spiritual needs.

9
Meeting Spiritual Needs
Sandra D. John

Assessment is an essential and often tedious step of the nursing process in determining spiritual needs, but it is only the preliminary step. Assessment is useful only if it leads to intervention. It is at the intervention stage that spiritual care often breaks down. Some nurses may intervene by instinct or compulsion, disregarding (or avoiding) thorough assessment. Others may carefully assess a client's spiritual needs and arrive at a nursing diagnosis, but never take the leap into appropriate intervention. Some guidelines may help to make the transition smoother.

1. Include the client in the planning. The client's freewill choice is crucial to the success of the plan. Include the care team in the planning, integrating spiritual care into the entire plan of care for the client.

2. Make short-term and long-term goals as specific as possible.

3. Plan an approach appropriate to the level of development and functioning of the client, using the framework, terminology and perspective of the client whenever possible.

4. Determine the appropriate use of available resources. The approach may include the use of prayer, Scripture, worship, religious ritual or symbols within the client's tradition and acceptance.

Assessment and intervention are cyclical, carried on throughout the nursing process. Thus a comprehensive care plan will include ongoing evaluations of the client's needs. Possible goals could include facilitating the following:

1. A connection with self. Integrating the isolated parts of the self and reducing isolation from others and from God.

2. Forgiveness of self and others for past hurts, living in the present and having hope for the future. Helping the client to develop a time perspective on forgiveness and integration.

3. A deep self-acceptance rooted in self-understanding and knowing God's view of worth and value. Fostering the ability to choose life in its fullness.

4. The ability to love, to have relationships, to be connected, to have roots and a home.

5. Being nurtured, being dependent in some ways, being parented.

6. Nurturing, being independent in some ways, being competent, parenting.

7. Conformity and rebellion, connectedness and individuality, being part of others yet with own personhood and ego boundaries.

8. Faith and trust enough to take risks, freedom from within boundaries, stability to make decisions and accept the consequences.

9. Worship.

The plan should include working out specific goals and walking through them with the client. The greatest resources are people—those involved on the health care team and the other significant persons in the client's life such as family, friends and the faith community. The most viable way this takes place is through the therapeutic use of self. Henri Nouwen says,

The mystery of life is that the Lord of life cannot be known except in and through the act of living. Without the concrete and specific involvements of daily life we cannot come to know the loving presence of him who holds us in the palm of his hand. Our limited acts of love reveal to us his unlimited love. Our small gestures of care reveal his boundless care. Our fearful and hesitant words reveal his fearless and guiding Word. It is indeed through our broken, vulnerable, mortal ways of being that the healing power of the eternal God becomes visible to us.[1]

Thus, in walking with the client in the process of establishing a healthier relationship with God and a more integrated lifestyle, the nurse incarnates the qualities the client needs. When the client cannot trust, the nurse can be faithful, be consistent, and follow through on commitments and time schedules. When the client is in turmoil and confusion, the nurse can demonstrate calmness and stability. When the client does not feel loved and accepted, the nurse can love and accept the client. When the client cannot feel forgiven, the nurse can show forgiveness and acceptance. When the client feels hopeless, the nurse can offer hope.

After an intervention plan has been formulated and implemented, continuous evaluation must be done so that the plan can be updated and adjusted. The following questions should be asked in the evaluation process:

Is the client participating in the plan?

Is the client correctly interpreting the intervention?

Is the intervention achieving the set goals?

Is the client moving from unhealthy to healthy religious beliefs?

Is the client moving toward authentic religious concern?

Is the total process of therapy, including the spiritual intervention, moving in the direction of integration for the client?

Hazel Thomas's story illustrates the principles discussed in this chapter for meeting a psychiatric client's spiritual needs.

Mrs. Thomas, a 77-year-old widow from a Pentecostal religious tradition, was admitted to a medical-psychiatric inpatient unit for an agitated depression with insomnia, anorexia and a forty-pound weight loss. Her chief complaints were a subjective feeling of twisted bowels and an inability to digest food. Medical evaluation revealed no organic basis for the symptoms. Her husband had died four months previously after a year-long illness during which she had given him total care at home.

Mrs. Thomas's religious concern first came to the attention of Janet, her primary nurse, during the initial nursing assessment when Janet inquired about suicidal ideation. Mrs. Thomas replied, "I wouldn't even think of that because I'm a Christian." When Janet shared that she was also a Christian, Mrs. Thomas asked her to pray for her healing.

As Janet began to know Mrs. Thomas she assessed her spirituality as the integrating factor in her life. As a child Mrs. Thomas, who had grown up in a strongly Christian family, had professed a personal faith in Jesus. The level of her religious concern seemed authentic; it functioned to give her hope and meaning in life. Janet had some clues that her religious life might be somewhat legalistic and guilt producing, however. For instance, Mrs. Thomas once talked about being told that if she had enough faith she would not be ill. At this point Janet had little other data about the correlation between her religious beliefs and her illness.

This was Mrs. Thomas's first psychiatric hospitalization. Twelve years previously she had had a similar condition that she believed was the same thing; she described both incidents as "collapsed nerves." Her developmental level, appropriate to her chronological age, was facing the task of old age of integration versus despair. A significant ego-function assessment and a mental status exam revealed a cachectic elderly woman with a sad demeanor who paced or lay in bed in a doubled-up position and who would not dress. Her thought processes were organized and coherent. She was oriented in all spheres with no hallucinations or delusions although she did describe a derealization experience. She expressed no suicidal thoughts although she had a concern that "I might not wake up every morning, and when I suffer so, sometimes I wish the Lord would just take me." She believed her illness was due to taking too many Anacin (actually only up to five a day) and adamantly denied that she was experiencing a grief reaction. Her reality testing was intact but with some impairment of sense of reality of her sense of self. She had been unable to function autonomously at home in caring for her daily hygiene and nutrition needs. Defenses being used were denial, regression, somatization, isolation and repression.

A beginning assessment of her specific spiritual needs showed needs for belonging, relatedness and love after her husband's death and her sister's return home, for hope, and for forgiveness of herself.

Janet examined her own motivation in making the initial assessment of the depth of Mrs. Thomas's spiritual needs. Although she admitted some desire to demonstrate to other staff the importance of spirituality, she felt her main motivation was concern for the client's wholeness and health to which her spirituality was central.

The team, consisting of the nursing staff and a psychiatrist, formulated the following plan:

Long-term goal: Return to independent living or residence with relatives.

Short-term goal: Relief of symptoms of pacing, insomnia, anorexia and derealization, with weight gain and return to doing her own activities of daily living (ADL). Behavioral goals included self-care hygiene with a shower every other day, gaining ten pounds, sleeping six hours a night, remaining out of bed three hours a day and socializing with peers.

The team decided, since Mrs. Thomas was distrustful of most of the medical and nursing staff but had begun to develop an alliance with Janet because of her Christian commitment, that Janet would do the primary therapy, trying to stay as much as possible within Mrs. Thomas's religious frame of reference. This would include daily one-to-one conversations from one half to one hour in length in which Janet would use a nondirective approach, sit with Mrs. Thomas in silence, or elicit description of current feelings or past events including life review. Janet was to look for clues as to feelings about her husband's death or previous grief experiences. Mrs. Thomas had become angry when staff told her that her symptoms were due to a grief reaction to the death of her husband and asked her to talk about it. She also felt pushed in ADL. Therefore, while the rest of the nursing staff were to be gently confrontive and to make requirements for her daily activities (dressing, sitting in the lounge one hour after each meal, walking in the halls twice a day, drinking three cans of dietary supplement a day), Janet would not push these requirements. Instead she would take a listening and supportive role, using prayer and Scripture as vehicles for hope and healing.

A major part of the care plan concerned further assessment both of the health of Mrs. Thomas's religious life and of her further spiritual needs. Janet's role was to be consistent, a calm presence, willing to understand and listen, quietly encouraging Mrs. Thomas to verbalize and grieve. She contacted the pastor of Mrs. Thomas's church and encouraged him to visit, which he did consistently, bringing news of church people.

Initially Mrs. Thomas talked very little, writhing and pacing with abdominal pain, but she did want prayer for healing. She showed her loneliness by not wanting Janet to leave at the end of the one-to-one sessions and by saying that no one could understand her. Janet's approach included reflection on how alone Mrs. Thomas felt, sitting with her in silence and praying with her for strength and healing "in all ways, whatever you know she needs." Mrs. Thomas gradually began to say that Janet understood her.

Janet found that her use of Scripture was especially meaningful. One day when Mrs. Thomas was talking very little, Janet began quoting Psalm 23 and Mrs. Thomas joined in. When Janet repeated Hebrews 4:15, about Jesus' having experienced everything we do, Mrs. Thomas especially resonated with it and said it helped her know that God knew how she felt. Mrs. Thomas then remembered Matthew 10:29 and frequently observed that since God knew when each sparrow fell, he was certainly aware of her suffering.

By the fourth day Mrs. Thomas began to talk more. At various times she began to bring up past grief experiences in her life—the deaths of eight siblings, a nephew, her parents. Loneliness was a consistent theme. It became apparent that she feared getting better because then she would have to go to a rest home, since she had no one to live with her in her own home and feared living there alone. Having no one to count on since her husband's death was a deep concern. When she felt hopeless it was because of the aloneness. Before, when she couldn't have faith for herself, she felt she had been healed by the faith of her husband, sister and friends, but now she had no one. Janet said she would have faith for her, and when she conveyed this to the team, others united in telling Mrs. Thomas of their support and prayers for her. Janet used the image of the four friends of the paralytic (Mk 2:1-12; Lk 5:17-26) and affirmed that she wasn't alone; others were willing to walk with her toward health.

Janet encouraged her when she showed interest in and was helpful to other patients, because this made Mrs. Thomas feel that she was as useful to others as she had been formerly. Visits and calls from her two nieces and church friends were encouraged.

Since Janet did not press her to grieve openly, Mrs. Thomas grieved indirectly as she verbalized images of feeling "empty inside, nothing inside, weak, melted, my body mostly dead." Gradually she began to talk about her husband's death, the year of caring for him in which she felt exhausted, angry and sad, her becoming ill during his funeral. Her prayers for him, she said, were the same as those for herself, either to be made well or to die without suffering. The expressions in Job 6:6-7, about food tasting loathsome, and Psalm 38:3, 7, about having no soundness in the flesh, spoke meaningfully to her and gave her encouragement that others knew how she felt. After three and a half weeks she was able to cry for the first time. This happened while she was praying and remembering songs that were meaningful to her such as "He Touched Me," "No Night There" and the songs at her husband's funeral. As Janet sang along with her and encouraged the tears, she began to identify her need to cry with her illness. After this, singing and visiting the hospital chapel facilitated her grieving.

Some clues as to her spiritual needs surfaced one day in the form of unhealthy religion: Mrs. Thomas began to say that certain people told her she wouldn't be sick if she had enough faith, so she felt she couldn't talk about her fears. Feelings of guilt and a need for forgiveness emerged along with clues as to possible ways in which religious practice may have contributed to the origin of her abdominal symptoms. A sister, more religious than she, consistently fasted and prayed and had been healed many times through this process. Mrs. Thomas knew evangelists who fasted or had abdominal difficulties. She felt she had "brought this on myself" by taking Anacin rather than trusting God. She said verbally she believed she was forgiven by God but had a hard time forgiving herself. When Janet prayed that day, she reflected on God's knowing we are earthen vessels (2 Cor 4:7), subject to many failures. She asked God to help Mrs. Thomas forgive herself.

Throughout her hospital stay, Mrs. Thomas participated in the plan and was given choices with encouragement. She said how prayers and Scripture met her needs. By discharge she had gained five pounds, slept through the night, sat up in the lounge up to three hours at a time, dressed daily, initiated walks, talked in the interview room rather than her room, and conversed with peers. She was able to be discharged to her own home with a person from her church living in with her and to resume contacts with friends at church. Mrs. Thomas became more able to forgive herself, express her emotions and take a less rigid view of God's requirements. She was able to reconnect with her faith community in the face of her loneliness over the loss of her spouse and to find hope for her life in doing the church activities that were meaningful to her. The nursing team agreed that the plan was successful.

10
Prayer in a Psychiatric Setting
Verna J. Carson

All too often the chronic wards of state psychiatric hospitals are godless places—characterized by an atmosphere of despair and hopelessness. The people who live on these wards are usually seen as incurable. Frequently they have been abandoned by family, friends and staff to a life of empty hours, interrupted only by television, radio, meals, sleep and an occasional planned activity. They certainly do not reflect Christ's promise that we should have life and joy in abundance.

I use several such wards as a clinical placement for my nursing students. While the students and I are on these wards we make every effort to meet the total needs of the patients including spiritual needs. We meet spiritual needs in a number of ways. For example, the students and I begin every clinical day with a group prayer. We ask for the Lord's blessing and his wisdom in our work with patients. We ask Jesus to allow us to see the patients as he sees them and respond to them in his love. We also pray for specific needs of patients and students.

After our group prayer, the students meet with their individual patients. The students begin and end each one-to-one session by reading a prayer and Scripture passage. The patients really enjoy the use of prayer and frequently request special prayer with either a student or me.

In addition, at lunch time I conduct a brief prayer meeting on the ward. Attendance at these meetings is voluntary; yet most patients come and participate on a regular basis. During the meeting one of the patients leads the group in saying the Lord's Prayer, another patient reads a Scripture passage, and I usually lead the group in singing a hymn. I also direct the group in discussing how the Scripture passage applies to life on the ward. I always allow time for each patient to make special prayer petitions. I end the prayer meeting by thanking the Lord for letting me share in the life of these and by asking the Lord to bless them in the following day.

As a result of these planned approaches to meeting the spiritual needs of psychiatric patients, several changes have been noted in the patients. For instance, the patients have a more realistic notion of what it means to live a Christian life. During our meetings they have identified the need to be kind and generous to one another—not only by sharing cigarettes and coffee but also by being understanding of each other's emotional needs. Another change is their greater awareness of the depth of God's love and concern for each of us. Probably because many of their prayers have been answered, the patients also seem to be more hopeful.

I am convinced from my experience that in *all* clinical settings, truly effective nursing care must embody Christ. Furthermore, embodiment of Christ must include not only kindness, love, skill and concern, but also an openness to talk about God, pray with patients and use Scripture passages.

With Psychotic Behavior

One day my students and I entered the psychiatric ward to which we were assigned and immediately knew something was different. Patients appeared physically unkempt and very agitated. Many were pacing on the ward and seemed unaware of the presence of others. Occasionally the sound of a scream pierced the already tense atmosphere. I noted the students drawing closer to me for protection, and I worked to maintain my outer calm. The staff informed us that the ward had experienced a severe disturbance, seemingly precipitated by a mass reassignment of men from one ward to another.

As an aftermath of this disturbance, several men were transferred to acute wards for observation and increased supervision. George, one of the patients who had been assigned to a student, was locked in seclusion for violent behavior. The staff advised us not to be alone with this particular patient. However, I knew the student has established a contract to meet with him, and it seemed important not to risk rejecting the patient by failing to appear for their meeting. Also, the student had been praying with this patient, and I believed that this was a time when he really needed prayer. Therefore, I persuaded a male attendant to accompany the student and me into the seclusion room.

Upon entering the room, we saw George lying across a bed, disarrayed and agitated. He immediately acknowledged our presence with a brief smile. I explained to him that because of his agitation we were not permitted to be alone with him, even though we wanted him to know we were interested in his well-being. Although obviously confused, he asked the student if she had brought the prayers with her. (Weekly I prepared structured prayers for the students to use with their patients.) The student acknowledged that she had, and she proceeded to read the prayer and Scripture passage to the patient. The patient then asked if he could keep the prayers. When we left the seclusion room, George was noticeably calmer.

Later in the day, I returned to the ward and was told that George was increasingly agitated and was asking for a priest. Since there was no priest available at that time, the head nurse requested that I spend time with George since I was so comfortable with the use of prayer. Readily agreeing to visit George, I found him thrashing on his bed and incoherent. As I sat by his bed I could pick up phrases such as "I'm no good" and "I'm rotten." His rambling speech contained many self-deprecatory comments, and he seemed to be feeling tremendous guilt for past behavior. I held George's hand and, after sitting quietly with him for several moments, asked him if he would like me to pray with him. After he said yes, I prayed: Lord, please help George to feel better about himself. Please give him the knowledge and assurance of your steadfast love and ready forgiveness. Please let George know that he is not alone. Please calm his spirit and give him your peace." As I continued to sit next to George, he became quiet and still and he squeezed my hand. When I left I assured George that I would continue to pray for him, and he smiled.

The next time I returned to the ward with my students, George approached me and thanked me for my prayers. During his meeting with his student he was able to discuss his inability to deal with stress, his acting out and his need for assurance about God's love for him. I was grateful that both the student and I had been willing and able to meet George's spiritual needs for an assurance of God's love, his acceptance and his forgiveness.

With a Catatonic Patient

Another day, as I listened to morning report, I heard that one of our younger patients, Bob, had withdrawn into a catatonic stupor. This regressive behavior disturbed me because I had been working closely with Bob, and I thought he was making progress. I wondered what had happened to precipitate this change, and I felt uneasy about my next approach to Bob. As soon as I was able, I went to see him. I found him lying flat on his back and holding himself rigid. He was staring at the ceiling with wide, unblinking eyes. He seemed to dramatize the expression "scared stiff"—he looked frightened and very vulnerable.

I sat by his bed and remained quiet for a time. He did not acknowledge my presence. After a few minutes, I began to talk to Bob. I told him that I was concerned about him and that although I wanted to help him, I felt powerless to do anything since I knew nothing of what he was experiencing. I asked him if he would like to talk and he did not respond.

The thought occurred to me that he might be able to communicate nonverbally. Therefore, I suggested that he could answer my questions without talking by blinking his eyes for "yes" and squeezing my hand for "no." To my amazement, he blinked his eyes. Just to be sure he was really in agreement with my plan, I asked him to squeeze my hand, which he did. With this system established, we proceeded to talk in a limited fashion. I found that Bob did indeed feel afraid, but he was unsure of what frightened him. He felt the need to totally control himself by not talking and by remaining physically rigid. He also told me he did not want me to leave.

After we continued in this manner, I asked Bob if he would like me to pray with him. He blinked his eyes! I proceeded to pray: "Jesus, remove the burden of fear from Bob and replace it with your holy peace and love. Let Bob turn to you rather than withdraw into himself, and let him experience the power of your healing in his heart, mind and spirit." Afterward I stayed with Bob for a brief time and then returned frequently during the day. His condition remained unchanged. However, the next day I found Bob walking around and talking freely. He thanked me for my presence and for my prayer and said that both had helped him.

I praised and thanked the Lord for using his power to penetrate Bob's catatonic withdrawal. This experience confirmed for me the need to share God's love with those patients he entrusts to my care.

11
Use of Scripture
Sandra D. John

Paulette, 57, became paraplegic following blood clots on her spinal cord seven years ago. Her history before the injury was unclear, but she apparently had a chronic thought disorder. Since the injury she has suffered severe bouts of depression including extreme psychomotor retardation, several suicide attempts, and feelings of guilt and helplessness. At times she has a healthy relationship with God, but during times of depression she feels abandoned by him and very sinful. One day she told the nurse she was paralyzed because she did not believe in God enough or love him enough. She based this on her understanding of Psalm 91:14-15:

Because he cleaves to me in love, I will deliver him;
    I will protect him, because he knows my name.

When he calls to me, I will answer him;
I will be with him in trouble, I will rescue him and honor him.
She reasoned that she did not love God enough since she hadn't been "rescued" and "delivered" from the paralysis.

What is Paulette's spiritual need? Is her use of Scripture a help or hindrance in meeting it? If it is a hindrance, how could a nurse help her discover a more adaptive use of Scripture?

The same questions may be asked of Mary.

Mary, 29, is in the process of separating from her husband, yet she wants to save the marriage. She is participating in both marital and individual therapy. In an individual session she shared with the clinical nurse specialist that she had been a "ten-month baby" and that she had a recurrent dream about going down a ladder into a hole filled with dinosaurs. "I don't think I wanted to be born," she said. "I think the world is too much for me." At the next session the counselor shared Psalm 22:9-10 with Mary. Mary was overjoyed because she had found Psalm 71:5-6 in her own devotions that week and had been eager to share the text with her counselor. These verses contain similar ideas about being God's from the womb and being kept safe as a child, with God present from the moment of birth and even before. These verses gave Mary much comfort and hope in her healing process. Mary and her counselor prayed together consistently in their sessions and used a healing-of-memories process in working through Mary's feelings.

The impetus or rationale for the use of Scripture in responding to the spiritual needs of the psychiatric client may come from either the client or the nurse. The client may initiate discussion by citing a Scripture passage or theme which influences his or her feelings, thoughts and behavior, or by requesting a Scripture passage for a certain need; or the nurse who has developed a relationship with the client may assess that in the person's religious framework the use of a Scripture passage or theme might be helpful and healing.

It is relevant and important to ask what clients are thinking and feeling when they ask about a Scripture passage. For example, when Beth asked if Judas was going to hell because he committed suicide, the nurse asked her reason for asking and assessed Beth's suicide potential. Likewise, when Kathy, after reading the account of Abraham offering Isaac as a sacrifice, set the garage on fire with herself and baby inside as a "burnt offering," the nursing staff had clues about her concrete thought processes and her view of God. When Frank asked about original sin and Romans 5, the nurses learned in dialogue that he was really asking, "Does God care about *me?*"

The nurse who believes that the Bible is God's communication with us—that it speaks to us of who God is, who we are, our human needs, and how our feelings, thoughts and behaviors can be made whole and healthy in a relationship with God—will seek ways to use Scripture in meeting spiritual needs. To be effective, Scripture must be used carefully. I have found the following principles to be helpful in determining how and when to use Scripture with psychiatric clients.

1. The Scriptures must be viewed in their total context, the individual verses or sections seen in light of what the chapter, the book and the entire canon of Scripture are saying.

2. Scripture speaks in themes or principles that give insights into our relationship to ourselves, others and God. It speaks to both our "being" and our "doing" in the world, both to who we are and to what we do. The theme of covenant relationships seems particularly applicable to the care of persons. One pastoral counselor identified the following biblical themes as relevant in pastoral care: (a) initiative and freedom, (b) fear and faith, (c) conformity and rebellion, (d) death and rebirth, and (e) risk and redemption.[1]

Ann, a 38-year-old divorced woman, was experiencing acute anxiety which included the delusional system that her father must die this week, and that right after his death Jesus would return on a certain day which was Passover, Maundy Thursday, Buddha's birthday and a full moon. She professed to be a believer in Jesus and yet was filled with terror that because of her sins the "end of the world" would mean salvation for the rest of the people, whom

God loved, but not for herself. She openly acknowledged focusing on Scripture passages about judgment.

The nurse listened to her, reflected her feelings of fear, sadness and exhaustion, and talked with her about guilt, self-hatred and the relationship with her father that lay behind the present fears. Then the nurse used Scripture in a thematic way. First she assessed that Ann gave high credence to Scripture. Then, in moments when she could hear and accept it, the nurse spoke to her of the thrust of Scripture, which is forgiveness, love and removal of fears.

3. Individual passages or books are to be studied according to sound biblical exegetical principles. One needs to ask why a book was written, to whom, by whom, when and under what circumstances. Knowing the type of literature a particular book represents is important. For example, historical books such as Samuel or Kings narrate events; poetry such as the Psalms express the feelings, praise and struggles of the writers; and epistles such as Paul's letters were written as instruction and encouragement in a particular circumstance. Therefore, a modern reader who wants to make personal application for today must first study the meaning of the passage at the time it was written, and then faithfully and prayerfully apply it to present circumstances.

4. Finally, we modern readers must make personal application and experience Scripture in our own lives for it to be meaningful. If Scripture is treated like a dead document, it will not be helpful to today's problems. It must be made relevant to people's lives. For example, the themes of God's concern for order, organization and healing might be experienced as one asks oneself, using the Genesis creation account, "What is 'without form and void' in my life?" "How do I sense God's working to bring order in the midst of chaos for me?" Or again, using Luke 13:10-17 where Jesus heals the woman with the flow of blood, one might ask, "How am I bound? When did this occur? How do the word and touch of freedom and healing come from Jesus to me?"

The nurse's attitude and motivation are paramount in meeting clients' spiritual needs. Certain guidelines are important as the nurse examines her use of Scripture. Scripture must be humbly used in a pastoral way to comfort, strengthen and encourage another rather than in a penal way to punish or judge. The nurse must not try to manipulate, control or have power over another by the use of Scripture. Scripture, though authoritative, is not to be used in an authoritarian way.

If a nurse's motivation is to encourage health, Scripture may help regulate a client requiring external controls while inner ones are being rebuilt.

Sally is a faithful Christian who studies the Bible regularly. During the manic phase of her bipolar illness, she played gospel music loudly all night in the halfway house where she lived in an attempt to present Jesus to her friends there. John 1:14 helped her regain control and consideration for others by helping her realize that Jesus was full of grace and truth, and that her actions were not presenting the truth very graciously.

We must be careful not to use Scripture out of our own need or compulsion to supply a quick answer to the client's uncertainty and anxiety or to summon external authority whenever we feel weak, helpless or threatened.

One client put a Bible under his pillow in order to gain insights as he slept; another requested a Bible as a good luck charm. Such magical use of Scripture negates human responsibility in choices and actions.

Scripture must not be used in a rote, ritualistic way without meaning. However, when a ritualistic use provides meaning and comfort because of familiarity, it may be helpful.

Mr. Henderson, a 70-year-old widower, was admitted to the psychiatric unit because the nephews with whom he lived were no longer able to care for him. He had some paranoid ideas when feelings of loneliness and abandonment reached proportions he could not tolerate, but most of the time he was in touch with reality and sat quietly in his room. He had believed in God's faithfulness all his life, and every day he asked the nurse to read him the

Twenty-third Psalm because his poor eyesight prevented his reading it for himself.

Scripture must be applied individually to the person and the situation. The nurse must know both the client and the Scripture well, and match them precisely. Timing is crucial. Scripture is always true, but its application may not always be helpful. Premature use of Scripture may have a Band-Aid effect on an outward problem without speaking to a real need further below the surface.

Betty, a middle-aged woman with a schizophrenic diagnosis, had been extremely agitated one night, sleeping hardly at all. When bedtime came the following night, Betty said she wanted to sleep. The nurse, who had previously spoken with her about her Jewish faith, suggested that the Psalmist had similar concern and read her Psalm 4. Betty was touched by the nurse's concern and appreciated her use of Scripture that was meaningful to her. She wept softly. The nurse later reflected that she believed the use of the passage had strengthened their relationship, building further rapport between them, although the Scripture alone did not address the needs behind the agitation and wakefulness the night before.

Donna, a young woman with a borderline diagnosis, was in the stage of feeling extreme anger toward her parents for her perceived abandonment by them. At this time she was also seeking to find a new center of meaning in her life. She began to visit churches and to ask about God's relationship to her. One evening Donna, sobbing uncontrollably, cried out, "Has God deserted me, too?"

Harold, her primary nurse, had been sitting with her quietly, allowing her to express her feelings. In answer he quietly read Psalm 27:10 to her. She stopped crying and asked in amazement, "Is that true? Does God know how I feel? Can I tell God?" Harold assured her he believed it was true and that she could cry out to God. He read Psalm 130 to her. She then asked, "Is God really on my side?" Harold quietly read Romans 8:31-39. After this,

Donna was able to talk calmly about dealing with her parents and seeking out friendships in the church.

Mattie, an elderly woman, was to be transferred from the psychiatric unit to a nursing home the next day. Feeling rejected by her family and fearful of the unknown, she said to her nurse, who knew about her strong faith, "I won't know anybody there, and I'll be alone. I just want to know for sure God will go with me." The nurse talked with her about her feelings in facing the unknown and going to a new place alone. Then she read Psalm 139. Mattie said some enthusiastic "Amens" and said she felt comforted.

Scripture will probably be unhelpful when the person is experiencing difficulty with thought processes, thinking concretely rather than abstractly or symbolically. Scripture may feed into delusional thinking. For instance, Jerome thought he was Jesus Christ and claimed that the New Testament was his autobiography.

Scripture can also be unhelpful when a person reads selectively from passages which reinforce self-condemnation. For example, Evelyn would read passages about judgment over and over. She chose Matthew 25 as the "most important passage in the Bible" and constantly referred to herself as a "goat." She told a nurse, "I know God sees me as a goat and will send me to hell." She was unable to accept passages about forgiveness and love, stating that they were for "other people who are sheep."

In situations where the Bible is being misinterpreted and seems to be exacerbating a client's illness, it may be more therapeutic to temporarily remove Bibles and other religious material. When the client becomes able to understand Scripture more rationally and appropriately, portions of the Bible can be gradually introduced and discussed.

In many situations, the Bible can be a positive therapeutic tool. Identification passages are often especially useful for persons who can find comfort and encouragement in knowing that people in the Bible also experienced depression, anxiety and fear. Mike was one such person.

Mike, 29, was admitted to the psychiatric unit for control of violent impulses which arose following the murder of his therapist six weeks before. He expressed rage at having been rejected as a child by his father, who could not accept his having cerebral palsy. He was also angry with God for allowing Gwen, his therapist, to be killed. He was afraid it was a sin to be angry at God. He was raised a Roman Catholic, and his faith had been extremely meaningful to him until now. In the last two months he had been to Mass only once, and then felt too angry to stay. Four years ago when a friend of his committed suicide, he had felt the same mixture of anger and guilt he felt now. He sometimes felt like killing anyone who taunted him for having cerebral palsy or who reminded him of Gwen's murderers. Sometimes he wanted to kill himself to be with her. He yelled, "God, you'd better do something *now!*"

George, his nurse, allowed Mike to express his feelings of hurt, anger, grief and guilt. He told him briefly that it is okay to be angry with God, that one can be angry only when there is a caring relationship. If we don't care, we have not invested enough to be angry. Anger keeps a relationship going. George told Mike about Moses' being angry with God (Num 11:10-15) and yet being called God's friend (Ex 33:11-23); about Job's arguing with God and God's response that Job was the one who had spoken rightly; and about the psalmists' expressing anger freely to God (Psalms 10, 13, 22, 77, 142 illustrate this, although in the situation no reference was given).

Wayne Oates summarizes the essentials of faithful use of Scripture in responding to personal needs: "Careful selection, effective reading, and vital relief . . . are the three necessities in the use of the Bible as a book of comfort."[2] This includes both Scripture used directly with a client and Scripture informing and molding the nurse's own life as he or she demonstrates acceptance and love for the client, acts graciously and forgivingly, exhibits calmness and order, and encourages trust and risk taking.

12
Clergy as Colleagues
Mertie L. Potter

Picture yourself working in an inpatient psychiatric setting. How would you respond to the following situations?

Sally, 17, who experiences periods of confusion as a result of drug abuse, comes to you and says, "My boyfriend says we should have sex. It's against my religion. What should I do?"

Chaplain Smith has just left the unit after visiting with Janet, 30, who frequently tries to manipulate others. Janet states, "I want you to call my own minister and tell him to get over here right now. I don't want to see that hospital chaplain ever again."

Dan, a 56-year-old widower who is struggling with depression related to his wife's death, tells you, "I'm a rotten person. God is going to send me to hell."

Is there a spiritual need in any of the above situations? How would you discern that? Is intervention on your part necessary? Would you involve a hospital chaplain in any of those situations? What would be your rationale for involvement or noninvolvement of clergy?

Clergy may be available in the work setting to help the nurse discern and respond to situations such as the above. This availability may exist whether the nurse is in an inpatient or an outpatient setting.

The Nurse's Involvement of Clergy

Whenever a spiritual need is evident in a client's illness, the clergy can be a valuable resource. To many nurses, the clergy seem to be the most obvious persons to provide spiritual care. Often, calling the chaplain is a way to avoid dealing with religious ideation. Other nurses see the clergy as intruders, especially if they have had negative experiences in working with a chaplain or a member of the local clergy.

Most clergy graduating from seminary in recent years receive excellent training in counseling and working with psychiatric clients. Many seminarians spend at least one quarter in Clinical Pastoral Education, often in a psychiatric hospital. Chaplains in psychiatric hospitals receive extensive training in providing therapeutic spiritual intervention. By including clergy in the care team, we can provide more comprehensive spiritual care.

In order to work effectively with clergy, it may be necessary to clarify role expectations of the nurse and the clergy in meeting spiritual needs. These expectations may vary from situation to situation, but should be mutually agreed upon. When I was head nurse on a psychiatric ward, I was told that one of the hospital chaplains was coming to see a client. The chaplain approached the staff in a disgruntled manner and demanded to know where the client's chart was. He informed the staff that he was the client's primary therapist, and stated that the chart should always be available to him. My role expectations for the chaplain were totally incongruent with his role performance. I was reluctant to contact that chaplain in future situations.

Other factors may also affect working relations with clergy. A nurse's educational background affects intervention. Students who have been told not to discuss religion or politics with their clients are likely to adhere to that admonition in their practice. Most nursing students are not taught how to assess and plan intervention for clients' spiritual needs. Unfortunately, many nurses feel spiritual needs belong to clergy alone. Furthermore, they may not know how or when to make referrals to clergy or how to work effectively with clergy.

"Territorial rights" may also enter in. Ward nurses responsible for client care twenty-four hours a day may become possessive of clients and not be receptive to "off-ward" clergy.

Another key factor is a nurse's personal relationship with hospital clergy. The nurse's belief system may be different from the chaplain's. In fact, the Christian nurse may work with non-Christian clergy or with clergy who profess Christianity but do not seem to practice it. Acceptance and respect between the nurse and hospital clergy are mandatory if clients are to receive optimal care for their spiritual needs.

Working with Clergy

A basic principle for working constructively in any relationship is establishing it well initially. This holds true for the relationship between the nurse and clergy. Rapport needs to be developed, boundaries need to be established, roles clarified, and strengths and weaknesses defined. Responsibility for initiating this relationship belongs to both nurses and clergy. Depending upon the level of commitment between a nurse and a chaplain, further benefits may follow. For example, in an outpatient setting, a pastoral counselor and I met weekly for prayer, sharing and supervision. We prayed for one another, our clients and the work we were doing with the clients. Our meetings were a time of encouragement and direction for us both.

Both encouragement and appreciation need to be verbalized between nurses and clergy. Both are often forgotten. However, they do not take much time and they have important positive effects, such as increasing one another's motivation and improving each other's self-esteem.

A nurse may be willing to work with hospital clergy but not know when to do so. Circumstances in which the nurse should contact clergy may vary with individual clients. However, situations like the following are generally appropriate for contacting clergy:

1. The client directly requests to see clergy.
2. A client indicates indirectly a need to see clergy (e.g., the client expresses confessional or spiritual reassurance needs).
3. The nurse is unfamiliar or uncomfortable with a client's faith or expressed need.
4. Staff expresses need for clergy (for example, as a spiritual consultant at the death of a client or at other crisis times).
5. The authoritative role of an ordained clergyperson is needed.
6. Sacraments or other ecclesiastical functions are involved.
7. Any other situation mutually recognized by the nurse and hospital chaplain to require contacting clergy.

The nurse's assessment plays an important role in this decision. Consider the following two examples:

Steve, 26, was burdened with guilt related to an incident in his past. He had prayed for forgiveness and had confessed his past to his pastor but had difficulty feeling forgiven. He struggled with the need to confess his past and wondered if he would feel forgiven if he confessed it again to a chaplain. (He had confessed to the chaplain earlier that day.) The nurse talked with Steve about his need to confess his past repeatedly and shared with Steve insights from Scripture related to confession and forgiveness. Steve decided that his confession and forgiveness were between God and himself and that he was forgiven even if he did not feel forgiven. The chaplain was not called.

Dick, 37, felt he was unworthy to serve in his church. He thought his minister would not want him to serve, because he wasn't "good enough." The nurse explored with Dick his feelings of worthlessness and his assumptions about his minister. The nurse encouraged Dick to talk with his minister about his feelings and to ask his minister about service opportunities in the church. The nurse called the minister and suggested that a visit might be helpful.

Opportunities to work with hospital clergy are usually available but often overlooked. You may want to consider utilizing the following tools, if they are available in your work setting:

1. Staff orientation programs.
2. Client referrals and follow-up of referrals to clergy.
3. Ward visitation, worship services and other clergy-run programs.
4. Grand Rounds for hospital staff.
5. Clinical Pastoral Education (CPE) programs.
6. Research.

For example, a hospital chaplain and I are planning to work together developing a Grand Rounds on "Spiritual Care." I have also been invited to share in a class of student chaplains on the topic "Nurses as Colleagues." I have a strong working relationship with a hospital chaplain, so when I was formalizing my thoughts for research on religious delusions, I conferred with him several times.

Nurses can be valuable resource persons to clergy in local community churches. Many clients with emotional needs initially contact their pastors. The nurse may want to be available to such clergy for information, education and consultation regarding mental health and spiritual needs.

If the nurse is working with a client who wants to talk with clergy outside the nurse's work setting, the nurse should encourage the client to contact the desired clergy whenever this is feasible and appropriate. The reason for this is twofold: to encourage client independence and to maintain confidentiality. Furthermore, it is important that the nurse be understanding and supportive of visiting clergy, as some may be unfamiliar and uncomfortable if the setting is new or frightening to them.

The potential for having clergy as colleagues does exist. The responsibility for developing colleagueship lies both with the nurse and with clergy. However, since it is usually the nurse who feels more at home in the clinical setting, nurses may need to be more assertive in promoting that relationship. By working together, nurses and clergy can provide more consistent and comprehensive spiritual care than either could working independently.

Section 3
Personal Mental Health: How to Keep Your Own Sanity

13
Qualities of a Christian Counselor
Kenneth L. Williams

The counselor who wishes to employ a Christian approach to counseling will find that the Scriptures speak clearly to this issue. Two interrelated areas relevant to counseling may be found in the Word: the qualities to be developed in the counselor himself, and the specific methods which the counselor is to use in the counseling process. This article is not an attempt at an exhaustive treatment of these two areas, but it can form the basis for ongoing study by those interested in developing a successful, Christ-centered counseling ministry.

If counseling is to be your profession you will need not only these scriptural qualities and methods, but also thorough professional training in personality development, abnormal psychology, and so forth. However, this chapter is not for professional counselors only, but for any Christian who finds himself helping others. Such a helping ministry may develop as a result of circumstances and also because the person has the gifts needed for helping others. Those in need sense these gifts and feel confident in going to such a person to receive help. Whether one is a professional or not, the same basic scriptural principles apply. In the actual process of helping others, the professional and the lay person work under the same spiritual laws.

Whether or not a person has clearly defined gifts in the area of helping others, the Word indicates that each Christian is expected to have a part in the growth of others in the body of Christ (see Eph 4:12-16).

Qualities of the Counselor

God has built into each Christian the potential for realizing the qualities discussed here. Each of us is potentially able to "attain to . . . mature manhood, to the measure of the stature of the fulness of Christ" (Eph 4:13). Fortunately it is not necessary to attain to this level of perfection before God can use us in the process of helping others. The point is not that we must have each of these qualities perfected before being able to help others, but rather that they are to be seen as guidelines for growth in our lives. The person who recognizes needs in his own life, who is actively seeking to grow in those areas and who is actually experiencing ongoing growth is better qualified to help others in their quest for growth. Thus the emphasis here is not on *being* like Christ, but on *becoming* like him.

The process of becoming like Christ is active rather than passive. We are not to wait passively for God to change us magically without our active involvement in the process. On the basis of what he has already done for us we are to actively "put on" the qualities he wants us to develop, such as compassion, kindness, gentleness and patience (Col 3:12-14). We are told to put on the new nature (Eph 4:24). These commands demonstrate that we are to actively develop these qualities.

The qualities discussed here are attitudes of mind. God is concerned about our attitudes (Phil 2:5; 3:15), primarily because our attitudes dramatically affect the quality of our relationships. For example, compassion is more than an inner feeling about someone. Webster's New World Dictionary (2d College Edition, 1980) defines compassion as "sorrow for the sufferings or trouble of another or others, accompanied by an urge to help."

Here are a few qualities which are important for the effective Christian counselor. I hope that this list will stimulate further study of the Scriptures in this area.

Love (agape) is not a unitary phenomenon, but consists of many distinct characteristics blended together. First Corinthians 13:4-7 emphasizes seven positive facets of love and eight negative things which love is *not.* Some of the positive aspects are discussed individually below. However, the counselor should also carefully consider the negative things mentioned which are inimical to love: jealousy, bragging, arrogance, rudeness, self-centeredness, irritability and unwillingness to forgive. These characteristics will obviously hinder one's effectiveness in counseling.

Colossians 3:14 indicates that love is more important than the other qualities mentioned in the passage. Without it, other characteristics will be of little value. Indeed it binds together all the other virtues into a functional whole. We are to *put on* this kind of love. It is not a feeling which we passively wait for, but a conscious process in which we are to engage, regardless of how we feel at any given moment.

First Corinthians 13:4-7 describes how love behaves:

1. Is patient: Love tolerates weaknesses and failures without becoming impatient; is slow to criticize or give up when a person fails to live up to expectations.

2. Is kind: Love is sensitive and sympathetic to a person's needs; is willing to help in time of need; shows active interest in another's welfare.

3. Rejoices in the truth: Love takes pleasure in what is true and

right; delights in both telling and hearing the truth, even though the truth may be difficult to face up to.

4. Bears all things: Love is able to overlook faults; bears up under anything; is willing to face anything with no limit to endurance.

5. Believes all things: Love is always eager to believe the best of the other person; is able to truly trust others.

6. Hopes all things: Love is always hopeful in every circumstance and able to communicate this hope to the person in need.

7. Endures all things: Love gives us the power to endure anything without wanting to throw in the towel when things don't go as expected.

Wisdom from Above. God's wisdom, like love, is made up of several individual qualities, each of which is critical for the successful counselor. The seven qualities of wisdom listed in James 3:17 are as follows:

1. Pure (from *hagios,* holy): free from defilement; free from sins which would hinder God's free-flowing power in helping others.

2. Peaceable: able to maintain harmonious relationships; peace-loving, free from strife.

3. Gentle: not harsh or stern; tolerant of others.

4. Reasonable: approachable, compliant, open to reason, willing to yield; without preconceived ideas or prejudices.

5. Full of mercy and good fruits: rich in compassion and kind actions; eager to relieve distress while showing good will; tolerant of others' weaknesses and failures.

6. Unwavering: free from partiality or favoritism; not ambiguous or harboring doubts.

7. Without hypocrisy: sincere and straightforward; consciously dropping all pretense in order to be congruous and authentic.

Awareness of one's worth as a person. Jesus emphasized this with his disciples in Matthew 6:26 and 10:31. Paul prefaced his instruction to put on compassion with the assurance that we are chosen by God, holy and beloved (Col 3:12). Unless we actually experience our own worth as a fact, we will be hindered in our ability to put on the characteristics which make a good counselor. The person who cannot accept himself in certain areas will be unable to help others accept themselves, especially in those same areas.

A spirit of gentleness (Gal 6:1; Heb 5:2). This is the opposite of self-interest; it means not being occupied with yourself at all. It means temporarily setting aside your own interests in order to give yourself totally to the interests of the person whom you are helping (see Phil 2:3-4). This attitude is also set forth in 2 Timothy 2:24-25: The helper "must not be quarrelsome but kindly to every one, an apt teacher, forbearing, correcting his opponents with gentleness."

An accepting attitude (Rom 14:1-4). No attitude can destroy the helping process so quickly as a judgmental spirit which refuses to accept the other person. Approval of behavior must not be confused with acceptance of the person. We may disapprove of one's behavior while accepting him as a worthy, valuable person. In fact, until this acceptance is clearly communicated to the person there will be little openness on his part and little freedom for the counselor to confront him with his behavior (see Prov 25:12). A judgmental attitude hinders our ability to see things objectively from the other person's point of view. The "log" prevents clear vision of the "speck" (Mt 7:3-5).

Acceptance requires a conscious, self-sacrificing decision to give up one's prejudices, opinions and values for the time being in order to see things through another's eyes. Once we see from his perspective and communicate our understanding, it may be possible to bring him to a realization and acknowledgment of needs, accompanied by motivation to change.

Awareness of one's own vulnerability and imperfections. Counselors are to look to themselves, lest they too be tempted (Gal 6:1), and not give the impression that they are spiritually or morally superior to the ones they are counseling (Heb 5:1-2). Counselors do not need to hide their own vulnerability to emotional stress (2 Cor 1:8).

Methods of the Counselor

The Christian who counsels is not confined to one particular technique, but should become proficient in several methods described in the Scriptures, using them selectively depending on the needs of the person being helped.

The following list is not exhaustive, but it covers the principal methods of scriptural counseling. The person interested in becoming more skilled in helping others should use this list as a guideline for further, in-depth study of each item, with the goal of learning how to apply these specific behaviors in the helping relationship.

1. *Parakaleo* ("to call to one's side, to help"). This term often refers to the relationship of one believer to another. It is translated "comfort" (2 Cor 1:3-4; 2:7), "exhort" (1 Thess 4:1), "encourage" (1 Thess 5:11, 14), "urge" (2 Cor 8:6). Apparently several specific kinds of actions are subsumed under this term. Perhaps "calling to one's side" implies being and doing whatever is required to help the person in need.

2. *Pray.* Two aspects are emphasized in Scripture: praying *for* someone in need (Jas 5:16) and praying *with* someone (Mt 18:19-20).

3. *Teach.* We are to teach one another. Colossians 3:16 may imply a one-to-one basis. The Word of Christ is to richly dwell in us as we teach one another. Also see 2 Timothy 2:24-25.

4. *Listen to confessions.* In James 5:16 the command to confess our faults to one another implies the reciprocal obligation to listen to those confessions. This is an important part of the healing process, especially in the emotional area.

5. *Admonish* (see Col 3:16 and 1 Thess 5:14). The word used here is *noutheteo,* meaning instruction and warning, primarily with a view to things that are wrong; it is warning based on instruction.

6. *Bear burdens.* Galatians 6:2 points up the importance of bearing one another's burdens. Part of bearing a person's burdens is to allow him to share them with you, by giving him an opportunity to talk about them. Another aspect is seen in the use of the

word in Romans 15:1: "We who are strong ought to bear with the failings of the weak, and not to please ourselves." This implies an act of self-denial in putting up with another's weaknesses in a non-judgmental way, letting him know it is all right to share his burdens with us.

7. *Restore.* This word means "to make thoroughly right." In Galatians 6:1 it occurs in the continuous present, implying patience and perseverance. It describes the process of patiently and carefully helping a person straighten out the wrong or faulty areas of his life.

8. *Speak the truth in love.* Ephesians 4:15-16 counsels us to do this with one another in the body of Christ for the purpose of mutual growth "in every way." Often this means to give loving, honest feedback to the person in a manner that will stimulate growth in him. Perhaps you will be the first one to interact with that person on a truly loving, honest basis. And the more truth you must share with a person, the more love you must have in sharing it.

9. *Empathize with others.* Romans 12:15 tells us the importance of sharing in a person's negative and positive experiences—feeling with him. This dramatically demonstrates our caring. However, a balance is needed in this; we must not become so wrapped up in others' emotions that we lose our objectivity and with it the facility to help them see things clearly.

10. *Help the weak.* This word *help* means "to support, to hold on to" (see 1 Thess 5:14). Sometimes all a person needs in time of difficulty is someone to support him, to "hold his hand" through the trial.

11. *Stimulate.* Hebrews 10:24 says that we are to "consider how to stimulate one another to love and good deeds" (New American Standard Bible). The word *stimulate* means "to motivate" or "to cause to be excited about something." At times the greatest help you can give a person is to stimulate him into action.

12. *Build up.* As used in Romans 14:19, 1 Thessalonians 5:11 and elsewhere, this means "to promote spiritual growth." It is a broad concept that might well represent one of the primary goals

of Christian counseling, to be reached by applying other concepts discussed here.

13. *Be a model.* 1 Thessalonians 1:5-7 and Titus 2:7 illustrate the importance of being an example for others to follow in behavior and attitudes. Change and growth will be enhanced if the person can actually see the right behaviors and attitudes exemplified in you.

14. *Encourage.* In 1 Thessalonians 5:14 we are commanded to "encourage the fainthearted." The word used here denotes consolation and comfort, with a greater degree of tenderness than indicated by *parakaleo.*

15. *Strengthen.* This means "to fix" or "to make fast," and is used of establishing persons. In Luke 22:32, Peter was told by the Lord to strengthen his brethren (see Rom 1:11 and 1 Thess 3:2).

16. *Forbear* (see Col 3:13 and Eph 4:2). The ability to bear with someone, to endure provocation while suspending one's own negative reactions is important in counseling. This gives the person a safe atmosphere where he can be himself without fear of retaliation or rejection. In 2 Timothy 2:24 the word can be translated "patient when wronged." In 2 Timothy 4:2, where we are told to preach the Word, "convince, rebuke, and exhort," we are also told to "be unfailing in patience and in teaching."

17. *Correct.* This primarily means "to correct or instruct, as with a child." The verb is used of family discipline (Heb 12:6-7, 10). According to 2 Timothy 2:25 we are to correct with gentleness.

18. *Complete what is lacking in one's faith* (1 Thess 3:10). This seems to imply that first we must carefully explore areas of deficiency in another's relationship to God, and then set about to help the person mature in those areas.

19. *Consider.* This word is used in various New Testament contexts. It means "to perceive clearly, to understand fully, to consider closely." In Hebrews 10:24 we are told to consider one another thoughtfully for the purpose of motivating to love and good works. This important facet of Christian counseling requires

the counselor to give himself in order to come to a deep understanding of the person. In most cases it is impossible to know how to motivate another person effectively without this kind of understanding.

In addition to counseling methods mentioned in the New Testament, several are found in the Old Testament. Only a few from Proverbs are outlined here, to give the reader an idea of what to look for in individual study.

1. *Dispense knowledge* (15:7; compare 15:2). The wise counselor is sensitive to the right *time* (Eccles 3:7) and the right *manner* (16:21, 23) to impart knowledge.

2. *Speak a good word to the anxious* (12:25). In the Berkeley translation, a "kind word" is given. We can help others out of their anxiety by the use of kind words (see 15:23).

3. *Reprove wisely* (25:12). Note the two components involved in the process: the wise reprover and the listening ear. We must gain the right to be heard before reproof will be accepted.

4. *Help to plan* (11:14; 15:22). Helping other persons to plan sometimes involves giving advice, but most often the best way is to help them think through the implications of their plans by asking the right questions.

5. *Understand* (18:2). The wise counselor takes great pleasure in understanding others. This process requires the counselor to refrain at times from talking about himself and his opinions.

6. *Listen well* (18:13). One mark of an effective counselor is the ability to listen well—to truly hear the counselee out before giving an answer. Often the first things a counselee talks about represent only the tip of the iceberg, or possibly just a small unrelated piece of ice floating on the sea while the iceberg lies mostly submerged, waiting for an opportune time to surface. To listen intently while withholding one's own ideas for the moment is one of the most difficult skills to develop, requiring a great deal of self-sacrifice. Yet it is the sine qua non of good counseling.

Do you want to be more effective in helping others? Your effectiveness may be directly related to your ability to apply scriptural principles of counseling. Take time to evaluate yourself realistically with regard to the *attitudes* spoken of in Scripture. Solicit feedback from trusted friends and family, in order to see yourself in these areas through their eyes. Then begin to evaluate your performance as a counselor in the specific *methods* mentioned in this chapter. Choose one attitude and one method in which you need to grow to be more effective in your helping ministry, and begin to work on them.

14
Caring for Your Colleagues
Verna J. Carson

Bob came out of the team conference feeling frustrated and rejected. They were discussing a treatment plan for Mary Johnson, a severely depressed mother of three teen-age boys. Mary carried her Bible with her everywhere she went. She also carried an overwhelming sense of guilt, constantly quoting Scripture to condemn herself as "worthless" and "the chief of sinners." During the team conference most of the staff agreed that Mary's Bible and religious material should be taken away from her. Bob objected, saying, "I think her religious thinking and behavior can provide some vital clues to her depression. Perhaps we should let her keep her Bible and try to get her to verbalize what her faith means to her."

"Are you kidding!" a colleague exclaimed. "Her religion is

making her sick, and reading the Bible is just increasing her pathology. If we talk with her about it we'll reinforce her depression. I think we should wean her away from religion. Healthy people don't need that crutch." The rest of the team nodded in agreement.

One of the most formidable challenges for Christian psychiatric nurses is working with colleagues who do not share, or even respect, Christian beliefs. Tension often arises when we express concern for a person's spiritual well-being. In addition, the morals, values and lifestyles of most Christians are in direct contrast to the prevailing standards of secular society. This contrast can produce misunderstandings, hurt feelings and frustration.

How can a Christian nurse deal with this situation? Can we find a balance, managing both to meet high professional standards and to express our deep personal convictions in an apparently hostile environment? One solution might be to limit our associations to Christians, but that would be neither practical nor appropriate. Jesus expects us to serve him whether we are surrounded by a supportive community or stand alone in our faith. He expects us to be "salt" and "light" (Mt 5:13-14) in our daily circumstances, and he provides us with the grace to make a difficult task possible. I have found five basic principles which enable me to share my faith and convictions openly among my colleagues: I try to (1) be an excellent nurse, (2) be guided by love, (3) be consistently Christian in my behavior, (4) be earnest in prayer, and (5) be a gentle witness.

Be an Excellent Nurse
St. Paul exhorts us, "Whatever your task, work heartily, as serving the Lord and not men, knowing that from the Lord you will receive the inheritance as your reward" (Col 3:23-24). Although we are working for the Lord, the standards for professional excellence are set by human authorities. Nurses are employed to provide health care, not to preach. Our primary responsibility is to provide quality health care to our patients. A comprehensive care plan

should include the spiritual dimension, but only after careful nursing assessment.

Charles Mack, a junior nursing student, saw Mr. Sandler weekly in the mental health clinic for depression. In the course of the relationship Mr. Sandler told Charles that his wife had been hounding him to go to church. She told him that his present condition was probably God's punishment for his lack of religious commitment. In assessing Mr. Sandler's problem, Charles decided that the wife was probably right, but that her approach was wrong. Charles felt that he should try to convert Mr. Sandler. Each time Mr. Sandler visited the clinic Charles would quote Scripture and direct the conversation toward presenting the gospel. Mr. Sandler began to avoid Charles and refused to attend the clinic whenever Charles was present.

When Charles shared his approach with his peer supervision group, they criticized him for his lack of sensitivity to the patient's feelings of sadness and failure. As Charles's instructor, I strongly advised him not to use this approach, since it communicated judgment rather than love and acceptance to Mr. Sandler. I suggested that he could still pray for the patient, but that he should avoid forcing Mr. Sandler to discuss spiritual things. Instead of complying with my suggestions, Charles became more zealous and inappropriate in his witnessing while neglecting the basic principles of good nursing. By the end of his psychiatric rotation he had alienated himself from both peers and patients, but he felt very righteous.

On the other hand, competency in nursing skills provides the practitioner with the dual opportunities of serving as a role model to peers and of serving the Lord through ministering to patients. Alleviating others' pain mirrors what Jesus did when he walked the earth. Jesus not only concerned himself with people's spiritual needs, but he restored them to wholeness by healing their emotional and physical wounds as well. When a nurse recognizes the power in this ministry of healing, he or she becomes a vessel through which the love of Jesus flows.

Be Guided by Love

In 1 Corinthians 13:1-13 St. Paul describes the qualities of love and states that of all God's gifts, the gift of love is the greatest. Our relationships with colleagues must be characterized by love if we expect them to take us seriously when we tell them about the source of that love. In 1 John 3:18 we are commanded to "love in deed and in truth," and not merely "in word or speech." Loving in deed is an action response; that is, we *do* loving things for others. There is no end to the ways we can operationalize this commandment.

Geri Collins, a junior nursing student, was assigned to care for Anna Jacob, a patient in the seclusion room. Anna was a frightening person who had been placed in seclusion for striking another patient and screaming obscenities. When Geri went into the seclusion room she found Anna in a catatonic state and covered with feces. Realizing she needed help, Geri went to the nurses' station to seek assistance. The only nurse who volunteered to help was Mrs. Bechtel. Together they gave Anna complete care; then they worked out a schedule so that each of them would spend time with Anna to keep her from being alone for the rest of the day.

At the end of the day Geri said to Mrs. Bechtel, "You know, I was sick to my stomach when I walked in there. I don't think I could have taken care of Anna by myself. Thanks a lot!"

"To tell you the truth, I had to do a lot of praying to overcome my own attitude as we worked with Anna," Mrs. Bechtel replied. "I find I really need God's love to take over in situations like this."

Mrs. Bechtel was not uttering pious platitudes. She had earned her right to speak by her actions. She shared the source of her strength openly and naturally without preaching or self-righteousness.

Other ways of showing love to colleagues include remembering birthdays, complimenting them on jobs well done, and being sensitive to personal problems and concerns. Our ability to love our colleagues, regardless of their religious beliefs, is a direct measure of our ability to communicate the gospel to others. When we fail to love, whether by harshness, impatience, anger, gossip, jealousy or self-seeking, we block others' ability to see Jesus in us.

Be Consistently Christian

Romans 12:2 speaks of the need to stand firm in our faith and to resist the pressure to "fit in" with prevailing standards of behavior. There will be times when we will be questioned about our lack of participation in some things and our support of others. It is important that we be able to state our beliefs honestly without attacking other people or their beliefs. We should not be apologetic for seeking and following God's will, but neither should we dictate what is right for others.

Marie frequently arrived for work looking rumpled and exhausted. One morning she looked especially distraught. She confessed to Sue during break, "I didn't get home to change. I slept over with Johnny in the doctor's residence. I don't know how long I can go on like this—he'll never leave his wife. I think he's just using me."

Sue was tempted to preach. She was inwardly repulsed by Marie's lifestyle, but she silently prayed for the ability to listen nonjudgmentally. Over the months Marie continued to trust Sue and to pour out her heart to her. Finally one day she said, "I don't get it. You are the last person here that I'd expect to understand all this, but you really care, don't you? Your religion isn't fake, is it? Do you think I could go to church with you sometime?"

When we are dealing with colleagues whose moral standards are different from our own, we have a special responsibility to extend courtesy and love so that we can better understand them. We need to pray that we will be able to see our peers with the eyes of Jesus, so that our spirits offer love rather than judgment and condemnation.

Some of the common conflict areas where a Christian nurse will have to stand firm are gossip, jealousy, competition and dealing with an overly demanding superior. Our responsibility in these areas is clear-cut. For instance, gossip or malicious talk about coworkers or patients is wrong. We need to discourage it and refuse to participate. That is not always easy, because gossip is contagious. When possible, we need to counter the poison of gossip with kind words and positive insights into the situation.

A strong tone of derision prevailed at a unit conference when the nurses discussed Nina, a fifteen-year-old prostitute who was admitted with signs of physical abuse and sexual assault. She had been found wandering in a city park, barefoot, partially clothed, confused and incoherent. One of the nurses remarked, "I don't think we should waste our time on patients like her. We'll get her put back together again, and she'll go right back to that pimp." The others nodded in agreement and began talking about other situations which they felt supported their position.

It was tempting for Peggy to join in the storytelling. Her Christian values did not condone prostitution, but she realized that Nina would not receive proper care unless the discussion was redirected. Finally, she said, "It makes me uneasy when we talk like this about a patient. I think Nina is in a great deal of pain. It seems like she needs a structured environment that is very firm and very loving."

Jealousy, competition and conflicting viewpoints can lead to open warfare among colleagues. Christian nurses must try to respond to conflict by bringing reconciliation and peace. This requires an emotional neutrality and the ability to see value in each viewpoint in order to defuse situations and bring personnel back together in harmony. The risk of such a position is that we may become the object of attack ourselves.

Lois was always the peacemaker on her unit. She was also willing to tackle the unwanted assignments and difficult patients. She felt strongly that her nursing should reflect Jesus Christ, but it bothered her that the others called her "Supernurse." Lois interpreted the nickname as rejection, but maintained a loving attitude toward other staff members. When the position of head nurse opened up, a delegation from Lois's unit went to the nursing office to request that Lois be promoted to the position. "She is the only one we really trust to be fair," they told the Director of Nursing.

Dealing with a demanding superior requires that we first examine our own performance to make sure that our boss has no legitimate reason to be displeased with our work. Of equal importance is our need to recognize and to submit to God-given authority, and to perform our assigned job without complaint.

At coffee several nurses were complaining about the head nurse, who had been snippy and sarcastic all day. "She'd better not ask me for any favors," Donna asserted. "I'm not doing any more than I have to for her."

Joanne struggled with her feelings. She had been the brunt of some particularly cutting remarks from the head nurse that morning. Afterward, she had spent a few minutes in the restroom praying about it and had gained some new perspectives. "You know," she said to the other nurses, "she has a lot on her mind today. We have a staff meeting with the new psychiatrist, we've had two new admissions—both acutely psychotic—plus we had two staff call in sick. She was also on call for the whole building this weekend and didn't get much time off. I think we should give her a break and make a real effort to lend her a hand."

We need to see our superiors through the eyes of Jesus in order to see their needs, problems and pressures. Our willing service, offered without grumbling, may ease their burden. If we have specific areas of concern, we need to share these openly with our supervisors in order to resolve or prevent misunderstandings.

Be Earnest in Prayer

Ephesians 6:18 tells us, "Pray at all times in the Spirit, with all prayer and supplication. To that end keep alert with all perseverance, making supplication for all the saints." A quick prayer for a patient as you walk down the hall, a short time of meditation in the restroom, an appropriate prayer at a patient's bedside, a few minutes in the chapel before going on duty, or prayer and Bible study with colleagues over lunch or after work can be opportunities to walk in close fellowship with the Lord throughout the day.

We need to pray for each patient in our care. There may not be an appropriate opportunity to pray with every patient, but there is nothing to stop us from praying for them. We also can pray for the needs of our colleagues. Sometimes by letting our peers know that we are keeping their needs in prayer, we communicate caring even if they seem skeptical about the value of prayer. We also need to pray that God will strengthen our coworkers as they bring healing and relief to the afflicted.

Be a Gentle Witness

St. Paul wrote to Timothy, "The Lord's servant must not be quarrelsome but kindly to every one, an apt teacher, forbearing, correcting his opponents with gentleness. God may perhaps grant that they will repent and come to know the truth" (2 Tim 2:24-25). It is natural to become defensive and quarrelsome when a colleague attacks the Christian faith or religion in general. If we resist the impulse to fight back, we can usually gain a hearing by quietly and honestly sharing what the Lord has done in our lives, carefully avoiding preaching or judging. For instance, I could say, "My faith has been a real source of strength to me. It means so much to know that God cares about me personally. I believe that a healthy religious faith is essential to good mental health."

When the spiritual needs of patients are being neglected, we have the opportunity to become "apt teachers." We can begin by setting an example. For instance, when a colleague tells you, "Mrs. Colson talks about hating God and being angry with him for her frequent depressions," you could respond by offering to go with her to talk to the patient about her feelings toward God. When you routinely include a spiritual assessment in your nursing diagnosis, you provide a natural forum for discussion. If you are drawing spiritual needs to the attention of a skeptical colleague or superior, you must be able to present a thoughtful rationale for your assessment. If met with questioning or resistance, you should respond in a nondefensive and articulate manner. If forbidden to openly deal with spirituality, then you can only turn the situation over to God.

We can also be gentle witnesses by being sensitive to the needs, hurts and concerns of our colleagues. We can communicate God's love through listening and caring, offering to pray for them or with them, and appropriately sharing Scripture with them. Sometimes we will be blessed by having a colleague who asks to know more about Jesus. At such times it is important to have a clear understanding of the gospel so that we can explain it to the other person.[1]

In summary, we are witnesses to the love of Jesus and to the salvation that comes to us through his cross. However, if we are to draw people to Jesus, we must first recognize and communicate that our God is the God of love. All our actions and words should derive from this fundamental understanding as we strive to be ambassadors of Jesus Christ. Second, we must respect the choices and opinions of others. If God in his infinite wisdom is willing to let us choose not to follow him, then we should not attempt to coerce others into faith. Our responsibility is only to be gentle, faithful witnesses.

15
Are My Beliefs Unbalanced?
Sidney Whitley Langston

Betsy grew up in a loving Christian family. Her parents set firm limits, guided by a code of conduct taught by their church, and Betsy respected them. She seldom questioned the rules, since most of her close friends belonged to the same church and followed the same rules. But now that Betsy was in nursing school her values were being shaken, and she was in crisis.

It all started the first week of school. After attending a student-led Bible study, Betsy was horrified to discover that the Christians on campus were inviting friends to go with them to see *Chariots of Fire* as an evangelistic project. Even the thought of going to a movie sent chills down Betsy's spine. Finally she told the group, "Christians don't go to movies!" From then on, she refused to participate in any campus Christian groups and spent as little time as possible on campus.

Even nurses are not exempt from unhealthy religious beliefs. Betsy was basically a mentally healthy person, but her legalistic background prevented her from fully understanding God's grace. None of us holds a completely balanced set of beliefs. The apostle Paul tells us, "Now we see in a mirror dimly, but then face to face. Now I know in part; then I shall understand fully, even as I have been fully understood" (1 Cor 13:12).

Each of us needs to evaluate our religious beliefs periodically to determine whether they are biblical or merely cultural, healthy or unhealthy.

Look back over the continua of healthy and unhealthy religious beliefs on page 71, and evaluate where you fit into each column. Many Christians find themselves slightly to the right of center in each area. A great deal of available evidence documents that a strong religious faith and its accompanying values usually have a beneficial effect on a person's mental health.[1] On the other hand, a religious environment which constantly reinforces feelings of worthlessness and depravity can actually prevent a person from being able to hear the gospel message of forgiveness and renewal.[2] Such teaching may lead a person to accept Christ out of fear. The person may also develop a negative self-concept and be left with many distorted and unhealthy religious beliefs.

Even Christians from a healthy spiritual environment are susceptible to the same problems in life which beset our clients. We experience grief, doubt, sadness and interpersonal tension. We become discouraged, lonely and sick. In times of depression or in crisis, we may not be able to sense God's presence and care. Sometimes we can feel defeated by interpersonal conflicts, the pressures of life, or unconfessed sin. These pressures, coupled with lingering unhealthy religious beliefs, can leave us feeling frustrated and ineffectual. God can seem very far away. We can begin to tilt further toward one of the unhealthy ends of the religious beliefs continua.

Jan found that happening as she began her psychiatric rotation. One year before entering nursing school Jan was treated by a psychiatrist for depression, and she feared that the pressures of psychiatric nursing would set her back into the depression.

Jan grew up in a home where the children were sent to church every Sunday, but the parents never attended. Her spiritual training consisted of being told what a "good Christian" should and should not do. She came to believe that spiritual growth was measured by how well she followed these guidelines.

Her home environment was disruptive and chaotic, and she established little sense of stability and security. Her parents made heavy demands on the children, giving them tasks to perform and punishing them severely if they did not do them perfectly. Jan's parents communicated that they were always right, and they insisted that the children be "seen and not heard."

Jan developed feelings of anxiety, anger, guilt, insecurity and a low sense of self-esteem and self-worth. Consequently, when Jan graduated from high school, the crisis of embarking on a new phase of her life created feelings of fear, uncertainty and depression. She sought professional help and concurrently began attending a Bible-study group with a friend. Through the Bible study Jan gained a more balanced understanding of God and his love for her. Therapy with the psychiatrist lifted her depression, so she was able to accept God's love for her. She accepted Christ as her Savior and began a gradual process of maturing spiritually and emotionally. A year later she entered nursing school.

Now, as she faced a psychiatric clinical rotation, she questioned whether she would be able to help clients since she had once been mentally ill herself. Her old fears and feelings of inferiority nagged at her. She doubted and fretted over her ability to intervene effectively with a client, and she even claimed that she was not worthy to be a nurse. Furthermore, she felt she was not capable of meeting the objectives of this rotation, although she had been academically successful thus far. Jan came to me, her clinical instructor, and told me her belief that if she did not successfully meet the objectives, the school would ask her to leave. She conjectured that this would be punishment for not perfectly meeting the goals of the task assigned.

Finally, one day in tears Jan told me about her fears and apprehensions. I attempted to help her realize that she should be able to intervene very effectively and emphatically with her clients since she herself had received successful treatment for depression. We talked about the meaning of her salvation in Christ and how that makes her a whole and healed person. I shared several passages of Scripture with her. Then we discussed how she could successfully meet the clinical objectives. I explained that failure to meet the objectives would not result in expulsion or punishment, but rather would be understood as a consequence of many variables affecting her life at this particular time. In fact, Jan survived the rotation and did well in it.

Legalism and guilt feelings can cause problems, but they are not the only manifestations of unhealthy religious beliefs. Diane was a relatively new Christian. She was excited about her faith and tried to put God first in her life. She took seriously the statement in Philippians 4:13, "I can do all things in him who strengthens me." Instead of studying, Diane prayed and expected God to put facts into her head miraculously. After failing all her courses, Diane left school believing that it was God's will for her to fail. She moved back home with her parents and did not try to get a job, because she felt she should spend all her time witnessing to her parents.

Jack became a loner after most of his friends dropped him for his constant harangues about how Christ had changed his life. He attributed the rejection to "the offense of the gospel."

Eleanor was constantly injuring her ankle or knee or undergoing some sort of surgery. She never complained; in fact she seemed to enjoy the inconvenience, quoting Colossians 1:24, "Now I rejoice in my sufferings for your sake, and in my flesh I complete what is lacking in Christ's afflictions."

Unbalanced beliefs are not always that extreme. Each of us experiences periods when our faith is clouded by doubt, our self-images are dashed, we feel alienated and alone, and we expect God to do our bidding. It helps to take stock once in a while and evaluate whether our beliefs are properly balanced and biblical. Being in a healthy worshiping, nurturing, mission-oriented Christian community is essential for maintaining balance, and so are personal prayer and Bible study. In addition, we can take time occasionally to look at ourselves, our thoughts, feelings and behavior, to see if what we think we ought to believe is consistent with the way we live our lives.

Our religious beliefs permeate our whole being. Healthy beliefs free us to minister to other people and to communicate the gospel accurately. Unhealthy beliefs hinder our work, our interpersonal relationships and our self-concepts. Our effectiveness as caring professionals will be enhanced as we grow spiritually, enabling us to share God's love with clients, friends and others.

16
Burnout!
Mary Berg

I'd rather stay in bed and sleep than face another day," Joan confided. "First of all, the phone woke me up early. Dad said he was laid off and couldn't pay my tuition. I didn't know what to say. We chitchatted and he ended with a choked good-by.

"An hour later the phone rang again. It was Sue: 'I've broken up with Bob. I have to talk with you. Can I meet you for lunch?' I agreed—reluctantly. Last time she chewed my ear off for *three* hours. I know she's hurting and I really should listen, but I just don't have the energy."

Joan wasn't finished. "I snapped at my roommate this morning, too. She was playing some of her Christian records, and the songs just irritated me. I don't feel like praising the Lord. I don't have the joy, joy, joy down in my heart. But why was I so unkind? It's not like me.

"And it's registration day," she went on. "I haven't had time to think about classes. It will be tricky fitting in what I need next quarter. And what am I going to do when Jan talks all the time at Bible study? I'm not even fit to lead it today. My quiet times are about as dry as the toast I eat with them."

Joan was suffering from burnout—a widespread syndrome marked by physical, emotional and spiritual exhaustion. Accompanying the exhaustion are negative attitudes, low self-esteem and loss of care and concern for friends. Often guilt compounds the problem, especially for Christians.

Burnout is usually the result of several weeks or even months of an imbalanced lifestyle: energy output consistently exceeds energy input. Like a car battery that goes dead when the energy demand exceeds the supply or the recharger malfunctions, so our lives run dry when we fail to build into them adequate means for physical, emotional and spiritual recuperation.

Joan's burnout, for example, resulted from weeks of overloaded circuits. Friends dropped in constantly to talk over boyfriend problems or roommate tensions. Wanting to become a counselor and sensing a Christian obligation to help people in need, Joan often gave up needed study time to listen to them. A part-time job had demanded extra time from her while a colleague was out sick. Her father's job situation was another concern. Joan felt absolutely drained. All these demands on her time and energy eventually exceeded her resources to cope.

But how can burnout be avoided? Or, if we are already suffering from it, how can we recover from its effects? Scripture offers some common-sense advice which emphasizes God's concern for the whole person.

Elijah was evidently a burnout victim too (read 1 Kings 18—19) —and with good reason. First he confronted the prophets of Baal who arranged a contest between their gods and Jehovah. God answered in a mighty way by burning up the sacrifice on the altar and giving Elijah strength to kill 450 prophets of Baal. Next, the wicked queen Jezebel threatened to kill Elijah. So he left his servant behind, ran a day's journey for his life, sat under a tree, told God he wanted to die, and fell asleep. He was exhausted. Apart from some sort of emotional and spiritual burnout his actions make no sense. After all, given what God had already done, he had no reason not to believe that God could easily spare him from Jezebel's threats.

Interestingly enough, God didn't chide Elijah or rebuke his unbelief. Rather he set about meeting Elijah's immediate needs— rest, food, a new assignment and an added companion.

What God did for Elijah suggests steps which Joan and we can take to avoid or counteract burnout.

1. *Get adequate rest.* How much sleep do you need at night? I realize this may sound like your mother. But if you need eight hours of sleep and you have to get up at 6:00 A.M., you can't go to bed at midnight and get enough sleep. Go to bed at 10:00. Recovery begins with simple, basic things.

2. *Eat right.* Skipping breakfast to sleep, or lunch to save money, may deprive you of the energy you need to cope. Toddlers fuss when they get hungry. Adults can get cranky too. On the other hand, eating too much, especially high-sugar foods, can throw your energy level off—and you need protein, green vegetables and so on for emotional as well as physical stability.

3. *Take time out for fun.* Leisure activities provide needed variety in our lives. Fun electives or hobbies can change the tempo of our days. Robin, a senior nursing student, found an evening ceramics class a valuable diversion from the mental stress of studying and from the emotional stress of the pediatrics ward. Digging her hands into the cool clay and throwing it on the wheel allowed her creative streak to come out and enabled her to work through frustrations. Besides, the clay didn't cry as the hospitalized children did. It helped her get her mind off them.

4. *Exercise regularly.* Physical exercise rejuvenates. It also develops muscle tone, increases feelings of health, decreases fatigue,

works off tension and gives energy. Exercise alleviates the physiological effects of emotional exhaustion brought on by either positive or negative stress.

Tiredness may often be more mental and emotional than physical. When this is so, exercise may help more than sleep. It may seem to be the opposite of what you need. But you'll be amazed at how much better you feel and how much more soundly you'll sleep after a short jog, a game of racquetball or a few laps in the pool.

Tom, a social-work student with fifteen hours of field work per week, found it took him an hour or two in front of the TV each night to unwind and forget his clients. Biking the two miles to the campus and social agency each day proved to be therapeutic. He discovered that he could work off frustration that way, and by the time he reached home he was ready to make supper. This added an hour or two to his day for productive activity.

Positive stress—being excited about something good—can wind you up so that you need to work off its effects in order to fall asleep. I remember a dating relationship that had this effect on me. I liked the fellow a lot. Often after we spent time together I'd lay wide awake in bed recounting the evening while the hall clock struck each passing hour. Finally, I'd drop off into a fitful sleep. The next afternoon I'd be nodding my head. Eventually I decided to get some exercise following our next date. When we got back I (believe it or not) jumped rope until I was tired, then showered and fell into bed, dozing off quickly. Exercise helped me to work off my pent-up energy.

Negative stress (*distress*)—which arises out of anxiety, worry, hostility, anger or sexual tension—often results in a faster pulse, muscle tension and increased blood pressure. Though the stress may build up so gradually that you hardly notice it, the net effect may be the same as the stress felt when having to slam on your brakes to avoid an accident. Without some kind of physical exercise the body is apt to turn on itself in muscle aches, headaches or stomach problems.

Regular exercise (at least three times a week)—jumping rope, jogging, swimming or just good brisk walking—can add significantly to your sense of well-being, increase sleep and lessen tension.

5. *Cultivate a good support system.* We all need someone we can talk to when we're down or troubled. Someone we can turn to for help, counsel and prayer. Someone who's available.

I remember the first time I thought through my support system. Four significant friends were moving away. I ached inside at the thought. I asked myself whom I would turn to when they were gone. I started calling Ramona, a new acquaintance. We talked weekly and a friendship grew. Later, when my other friends were gone and my ninety-two-year-old grandmother died, I was able to share my grief with Ramona. She let me cry, and I was glad I hadn't waited until my other friends had left before I got to know her.

To build an effective support system you will need to nourish friendships with people who listen and respond to you. It takes time to build trust, and you will have to be willing to give as well as to receive. A good support system is made up of more than one person. Often a small group Bible study can function in this role.

If you don't have such a group now, ask God to give you one. He may have in mind some people you wouldn't ordinarily suspect. Be ready to share your struggles and your joys with such a group.

6. *Make time for God.* Quiet time spent with the Lord in Bible study and prayer feeds the spirit. It renews you from within and gives God a means to speak to you. Even in the midst of pressure, dryness and overwork, consider taking a half day for prayer. Take a Bible and notebook and get off by yourself, outdoors if possible or someplace away from distractions. Spend time reading the Scriptures, writing down concerns and thoughts, and praying. Allow God to speak to you.

Burnout is not God's intention for us any more than it was for Elijah. The means for prevention and cure are much the same, but prevention is always easier and better. Begin with the basics: food, rest and exercise. Seek to lead a balanced life of study, recreation, contact with people, and worship. Cultivate friendships to build your support system, and don't forget that God is your most important friend. His resources are available to you through prayer and Bible study.

Don't say, "I'll start after the quarter ends." Now is the time to begin preventing or treating burnout. Take care of yourself so others will not have to take care of you later or pick up your responsibilities. A little discipline now can increase your effectiveness for God over a lifetime.

17
When the Helper Needs Help

Barbara E. Nelson

How could it be? What happened? Why did I burn out after thirteen years as a missionary in Indonesia? How could I have prevented it? I was a woman of deep faith, serving the Lord in obedience to his call. I went to the mission field for life. I wasn't supposed to get sick. Were my perfectionist standards too high? Were my expectations of myself and others unrealistic? Was it my neurotic need for approval and my fear of rejection and failure that made me a workaholic? Why couldn't I allow myself to receive from others? So many questions.

Upon return to the States, I spent the first three months at home in bed isolating myself from everyone. I thought I was just worn out, in need of a rest. Not until I went to Cape Cod that spring did I realize it was more serious than that. A friend said, "Barbara, you're depressed."

How could a nurse not know that she was depressed? Did I need professional help? I didn't think I was that sick. What would my friends say? I would not tell them. I would be too embarrassed to admit that I, a Christian, needed therapy. I had been taught to rely on God alone. I should be able to get myself together through prayer and Bible study. My friends could hardly be expected to have the time and patience to listen, the wisdom not to judge, the objectivity and maturity to confront, and the insight and skill to diagnose the root of my problems and help me sort out over forty years of living. I knew I needed professional help, but where should I go?

God led me to the therapist that was right for me. I was taking a course called "Counseling the Adolescent" from Dr. Ray Pendleton at Gordon-Conwell Theological Seminary. In it we discussed adolescent rebellion, identity crises, and issues around relationships, vocation and feelings. It was Ray's sense of humor, warm friendly manner, spiritual depth and sincere compassion that enabled me to go up to him after class one day and ask, "Do you counsel adolescents in their forties?"

Why should I be embarrassed about being in therapy? Many of my nursing professors had their own counselors and were not ashamed to admit, when they had a horrendous day, that they were going to see their therapist after work. Even though I had the inner resources of the Spirit, I needed God working through another human being to whom he had given the gifts of healing. If I broke a bone I would go to a surgeon. If I needed a root canal I would go to a dentist. If I needed spiritual counseling, I would go to a spiritual director of some kind. I had emotional problems and needed one skilled in psychological counseling.

What is it like to be in therapy? It's like cleaning out a closet full of junk and treasures that have been tossed in over the years. There is so much clutter and confusion that you need to drag everything out into the hallway where you can spread it out, see what's there and sort out what you want to keep. Some of it you forgot was there. Some you put away hurriedly, some you shoved in in anger and frustration and some you wrapped with tenderness. The closet of the mind also gets cluttered and needs sorting out. Therapy is a safe place to take the lid off pent-up feelings, to dig up repressed feelings, to find worth among the broken pieces and to sort out the junk from the treasures. I was shocked and surprised at the stuff hidden in my closet—unresolved guilt and grief, resentful relationships and a whole range of unexpressed feelings. After sorting, you rearrange what you want to keep; therapy helps you sort, discard, integrate, and make room for more.

Dr. Pendleton told me that it would be a painful process, but he did not know how painful. It took courage to be honest, to admit to myself and to him what I was thinking and feeling. It was a shock to realize how angry I was and how afraid I was to express it. I began to realize that feelings were not good or bad in themselves, and I began to experience and express a whole new range of emotions. What a freeing experience! It was okay to be human and to be a woman. Sometimes it was like going to confession—I felt guilt removed, God's forgiveness and the ability to forgive others. I had new energy to reinvest in new relationships.

I was finding that I did not need to be alone to be spiritual; that growth takes place in community, not in isolation; that it is healthy to ask and receive help when it is needed. I found myself breaking out of the prison of living up to others' expectations. In dealing with the fears of failure and rejection rooted in low self-esteem, I decided to risk rather than rot. For a time I felt very fragmented, when the pieces of the puzzle were scattered over the floor like the clutter from the hall closet.

With the Spirit's guidance, evident in all our sessions, the puzzle pieces gradually fell together. I saw my past experiences fit into my future as a chaplain. I began to exercise and lose weight to feel better about myself. I also began to crawl out of my shell to reach out to friends for fun and fellowship. As I began to express my feelings, I even enjoyed a more intimate relationship with God through meditation and more spontaneous worship. Therapy had been an integrating process and I felt I had grown in all areas. I wanted to continue to grow but came to a point in therapy where we both decided we had gone as far as we could at the time.

My well was full and beginning to run over. I didn't realize how empty my well had been until I saw the water level rising—and it has continued to rise ever since. Growth takes time, and I need to be patient with myself. I'll try to keep my closet in order, though there will be times when it will be cluttered again. As I live on a higher level of integration and wholeness, new issues will arise. Coming back to therapy is not failure, but a courageous way of getting through the roadblocks to growth.

18
When the Hurting Hits Home
Laura Carlsen

One of the most difficult decisions of my life was to seek therapy for my little boy. Making this decision involved coming to grips with my feelings of failure not only as a mother, but also as a psychiatric nurse and, most important, as a Christian. In my heart I believed that my knowledge of psychiatry should give me methods to deal with my son's angry behavior. Yet every approach I used, from behavior modification to dietary restriction of sugar, failed miserably.

I turned to God continually, praying for healing for my son and for myself. God seemed to have forsaken us. When I prayed for greater patience, God allowed me to be tested to the limits of my endurance. I asked to be more loving and in response to this request God greatly increased the capacity of my heart. Yet in spite of all my prayers, my son remained troubled. Was I not "worthy" as a Christian? Didn't God hear my pleas? I was led to seek therapy out of desperation and a deep sense of failure, but the experience has taught me some important lessons. First, I learned that no one is immune to emotional problems—not even me. Second, I saw that frequently God heals his children through the loving ministry of a competent therapist. Therapy can be a channel for the power of God over emotional problems just as surgery or antibiotics may be in a physical illness. But taking that first step to seek help was awfully difficult. Let me give you some background.

My first pregnancy was delightful in every way. My husband, Jack, and I had been married for five years, and we were thrilled with the prospects of parenthood. We were both very much in love with David before he ever made his appearance into this world.

David's birthday was beautiful! I will always cherish the memory of that day. I was so aware of the awesome power of God in the creation and birth of this perfect baby—all 9 lb. 6 oz. of him—with red hair and blue eyes.

But my high spirits quickly ebbed away as I realized that my perfect baby seemed to be an angry baby. David cried a lot. In fact, he cried most of the time. Initially, he did not nurse well. He seemed to be easily frustrated and upset, and sometimes he was inconsolable. At ten weeks David had his first asthma attack. His wheezing and struggling for breath became an all-too-familiar and terrifying sound to us. The remainder of his first year was marked by frequent illnesses and extremely fussy and irritable behavior.

At eleven months David began to talk, and very quickly he was conversing in sentences—mostly negative ones. With his newly acquired language skills, he was able to articulate what before had been only angry nonverbal behavior. He also began to be physically destructive. For instance, he painted himself and his room with an indelible violet medicine, and he broke a twenty-gallon fish tank. However, we convinced ourselves that this was the "terrible twos" we had heard so much about. Unfortunately, for David the "twos" never ended. Although he gave up the physical destructiveness, his moodiness, angry actions and sullenness only intensified.

My response to his behavior was to "love" him out of his moodiness. I convinced myself that he would eventually respond if only I could be more loving and more patient—but he did not respond. Occasionally, as if a storm had subsided, he would be like a ray of sunshine, happy, bright and fun to be around. But these times only allowed us to catch our breath and to get ready for the next onslaught of hostility. I often marvel at my own self-control. There were many times I wanted to hurt David, but by the grace of God I didn't. This "perfect" baby had made me feel like an enemy in my own home.

Despite David's anger, there was always a vulnerability about him that touched my heart. I could see pain beneath his tough exterior, but I had no way to stop the hurting. No matter how David was feeling, he had only one response. Hurt, fear and frustration were all expressed as anger.

For five years, we continued to find excuses for David's behavior. He was sick or he was tired or his feelings were hurt. It wasn't until our second son, Kenny, was born that we confronted the reality that David needed professional help.

Despite all our preparations, Kenny's birth was traumatic for David. He seemed angry and hurt. He began to match his angry words with equally angry and frightening physical acting out. Most of this anger was directed toward me and his new brother. David rebuffed all our efforts to help him to deal with his feelings. Still, we managed to turn away from the reality that glared at us daily. We said we would give him until the end of the summer to adjust to his new brother. At the end of the summer David would begin kindergarten. We convinced ourselves that it would be easier for him to deal with Kenny when they weren't together so much.

Unfortunately, the summer produced no improvement in his behavior. In fact, he added new features like urinating and defecating in his playroom, systematically destroying his toys, stealing and lying. Every day brought a new and horrible discovery of something he had done. Yet we were not able to admit that he was crying out for help that we couldn't give him. I found myself praying constantly, beseeching God to show me how to reach David. Words are inadequate to express the anguish I felt for my child. Sometimes David would say, "Don't let me do this, Mommy —I don't want to do these things." I would hold him at times like this and assure him of my love, but I did not know how to stop his hurting.

I found myself reeling in anger at God, screaming at him that if he was such a loving Father, how could he let a child of his suffer like this? I know now that God was answering my prayers not with an instant cure, but with love, control and patience. I believe that God permitted our pain to intensify because it was the only way we would give David what he needed.

After David had spent only a week in kindergarten, I received a phone call from his teacher. David had cut another child with scissors, and he had stolen crayons. His teacher wanted advice on how to handle him. Since I was unable to provide her with answers, she suggested that we utilize the school counselor. Unfortunately, the counselor was too eager to see all of David's problems as a reaction to his new brother. She suggested a few behavior-modification techniques which proved to be a total failure.

Finally, Jack and I decided that it was time to take more definite steps. I called a Christian counseling center, only to be told that children were not treated there. Later, I discovered that this information was incorrect. It seemed that God had chosen another path for us.

My next step was to see our pediatrician, who after listening attentively to the behavior I described, gave me an immediate referral to a Jewish psychologist. I wasted no time in setting up our first appointment.

At our initial therapy session, the psychologist spent time first with David and then with me. After I had spoken to the therapist and described David's behavior of the past few months, he seemed surprised. His impression of David had been that of a cute little boy with a sweet and docile nature. He felt that the dichotomy between the David I described and the David he had met indicated that David was a "seriously disturbed child." Those words cut me like a knife and brought images to my mind of wild and uncontrollable people. The psychologist had put into words the deepest but unspoken fear of my heart. It took me weeks before I could say those words without crying.

We began weekly therapy where we dealt with many issues. First seemed to be David's anger at Kenny. David wanted to be a baby again, to be held and nursed. He resented any attention that Kenny received. The psychologist pointed out to David how much better it was to be the number one son who could do so much more than a baby. Although Jack and I had tried the same approach with David, he could not hear it from us; but from the psychologist it seemed to make sense to him.

After his anger at Kenny began to subside, deeper problems began to emerge. In David's five years he had not learned that there were negative consequences to his hostility. He had certainly been punished and disciplined, but my approach of "loving" him out of moodiness had only reinforced the behavior. I had effectively taught him that even bad behavior got positive results from Mommy.

I began to recognize that I was afraid of anger and would do anything to block its expression. I was too quick to forgive and forget. The psychologist taught me that I needed to act angry by giving David the cold shoulder and withholding my attention when he misbehaved. The results were amazing. David hated being ignored and would mend his ways for a smile.

The psychologist also helped Jack and me to look closely at what behaviors deserved discipline and what things could be overlooked. It was apparent to us that in our desire to have a perfect child we had placed some unrealistic expectations on David.

In the year and a half we spent in therapy, we learned that David requires a great deal of structure and consistency in his environment. Without this structure, he feels insecure and acts out in an angry manner. I have learned to recognize what a powerful tool I am in shaping his behavior. I am less spontaneous and more discriminating in giving David hugs, kisses and special treats. He knows now when I am angry at him.

The road to health was a painful, uneven path, but well worth the walk. We may never know why David seemed so angry at birth, but we have come to love his uniqueness without forcing him into our preconceived mold of the perfect child. He has grown into a happy, secure little boy, capable of both giving and receiving joy. And my feelings of failure have given way to a new appreciation of my mothering and nursing skills and, most important, of my relationship with Christ. God held my hand, supported me and strengthened me throughout David's therapy. He affirmed his love for me and my child, and he healed us.

19
Psychiatric Nursing: An Opportunity for Growth
Diana Krikorian

Tina wanted to get the most out of her psychiatric nursing experience. She understood the concept of the use of self, that it was the crux of psychiatric nursing. She also knew that in order to use herself, she had to know herself. This knowledge, however, was not without its attendant fears. "Working on myself is getting to me, though I'm not sure why," she said. "I guess I'm becoming aware of too many aspects of myself that I'm not happy with. I want to be honest with myself, and yet I want to avoid confronting myself."

She continued, "Letting someone really know me is something

I've always wanted, but I realize that for someone else to really get to know me, I've got to know myself—and that's what scares me."

For Tina, the psychiatric nursing experience was the beginning of a continuing process of self-awareness. "It's been so painful in many ways," she said. "In a way I wish it had never happened; but then again, I've begun to grow and change. I'm learning to disclose my thoughts and feelings—something I was deathly afraid of before."

Tina found that self-awareness can be threatening as well as growth-producing. Probably more than any other type of nursing, psychiatric nursing affords an intense opportunity for self-awareness. Perhaps this realization was why one student said that she anticipated her senior year, "but not with pure joy."

Self-awareness involves understanding and integrating the cognitive and affective parts of the self. About halfway into the psychiatric nursing clinical experience, Jackie, an honor student, asked for a conference with me. "I don't know what's happening to me," she said. "I'm realizing so many things about myself; I'm not sure that I even like myself. I shouldn't feel like this as a Christian," she sniffled through her wad of Kleenex, "but somehow I feel like I'm not good enough—like I should be perfect or something. I feel like I should always have the right thing to say to my patient. I'm beginning to realize that I seem to need to excel to be accepted. Maybe that's a cover for basically feeling inferior—and yet, I shouldn't feel like that as a Christian. Also I've always believed that Jesus is the real answer to all problems, and I guess I feel like I'm falling short not to tell my patient about him. Generally, I'm feeling somewhat unglued."

Jackie's "supernurse" tendencies were overlaid with her ideas of what constituted a model Christian. Intellectually she knew that perfection eludes us as humans. She was aware that Scripture passages about being perfect related to the lifelong process of growing into the maturity of God by the working of his Holy Spirit within us (1 Peter 1:15-16; 2 Cor 7:1). Nonetheless, Jackie's cognitive awareness of some biblical concepts did not eclipse the emotional discomfort of edging into new understanding about herself. She was beginning to realize that even as a Christian she had some unmet needs and periods of vulnerability.

In a study I conducted with a colleague, we learned by analyzing student responses that relating to a mentally ill person can be quite different from relating to other types of clients. The unmet needs of the client can serve unconsciously to mirror the unmet needs of the student. Since all human beings have needs that are not fully met, everyone has periods of vulnerability at various times and to varying degrees.

What alternatives do we have for dealing with our vulnerability? We can allow our unconscious, unmet needs to contribute to a counterproductive, gnawing anxiety. Or we can confront these needs and make them contribute to a substantial growth experience.

We know that our awareness of the unconscious is often restrained by a psychological defense system which protects us from the anxiety of facing ourselves, our unmet needs and our vulnerabilities. This unconscious process functions as a needed defense, but also as a deterrent to personal and professional growth. How can the balance be tipped on the side of growth?

Through the process of becoming self-aware, unconscious thoughts and feelings can become conscious. Once we become aware of these thoughts and feelings, we can convert stress and anxiety into energy for personal growth. However, in the complex process of developing self-awareness, two opposing forces are at work: one that decreases anxiety by *inhibiting awareness* (by use of defense mechanisms), and one that decreases anxiety by *increasing awareness*.

We might way that one's self-awareness is on a continuum between the need for a "tight" or for a "relaxed" defense system in any given situation or time. There will never be total awareness. The goal is developing higher levels of awareness. Students in the psychiatric nursing experience may be functioning at any point on this awareness continuum.[1]

Know Thyself

What is self-awareness? One definition calls it the process whereby one is able to get in touch with one's values and philosophy of life. This then becomes the basis for one's functioning, both personally and professionally.[2]

How do we attain and continue attaining self-awareness? There are more variables than we dare deal with in trying to answer such a complex question. However, two aspects of the process are *honesty* and *self-disclosure*. For the Christian growing in self-awareness, God as well as self and others are included in the process.

Patti had been a Christian for several years. Her values and lifestyle were radically changed as a result of a personal relationship with Jesus Christ. "I've grown so much," she said as we sat in my living room, chatting. "Psych nursing is okay," she continued, "but I'm really feeling uneasy in our small group."

"In what way?" I asked.

"A couple of know-it-alls in the group are really bugging me. They're taking over like bulldozers. I hate to say this, but I feel cut down by what I think are two high-class snobs. I know that as a Christian, I shouldn't react this way." There was a great deal of feeling in Patti's straightforward replay of her experience.

I asked a question which was not about the small group scene. "Patti," I said, "What do you think of yourself?"

"That's it," she said, startled. "That's where I think the problem is. Actually, I don't really think much of myself." She sat in silence for a few moments. "Now that I think about it, I probably put others down because I put myself down. I never thought of it that way before."

Through a succession of honest talks, Patti began to gain awareness of the relation between her thought patterns and her behavior. "Anyone who has it together seems to be a threat to me," she confided, "and I have a tendency to knock them." We were able to pray together with more understanding.

Patti began to see that her system of self-defense was defeating her desire for growth toward maturity and authenticity. She was also beginning to realize that, for a Christian, self-disclosure can aid the goal and work of the indwelling Holy Spirit. She was gaining a new perspective on the quality of her interactions with her peers in the psychiatric nursing clinical group.

Honesty and self-disclosure for a Christian student is no less difficult than for a non-Christian. In *All I Need Is Love,* Nancy Anne Smith attests to this. She relates the beginning of her breakthrough toward self-awareness when she was finally able to say: "Okay, Lord,. . . you already know how . . . I am, so I might as well get honest with myself about how I am and get honest with you. Help me to start right now to be honest about my feelings."[3] A similar theme is reflected in Psalm 139:

Search me, O God, and know my heart!
Try me and know my thoughts!
And see if there be any wicked way in me,
and lead me in the way everlasting! (vv. 23-24)

An individual's commitment to Christ does not preclude the possibility of having emotional needs.

Johanna had been married quite a few years when she confided, "In all these years, I've never been able to tell my husband that I love him; I just can't bring myself to say it." Johanna was raised in a heavy-handed patriarchal system. Tenderness and expression of feelings were seldom conveyed in her home. In fact, when they spontaneously emerged at times, she vividly remembered being cut down for saying such "silly things."

Now in her marriage Johanna, who is a Christian, finds responding to her husband's love less natural than responding to his demands. In fact she expects demands more than love. Her response to God is similar. She subtly punishes herself for not living up to what she demands of herself. She sees God, herself and others in terms not of love but of demand. Genuinely accepting and giving love are foreign to her.

Johanna's developmental history cannot be erased, but she can choose to view it as an opportunity for growth and maturing. Pain of any kind (physical, emotional, spiritual) has the potential to produce growth, though knowing this doesn't make pain any easier to live through.

Although the spiritually and mentally healthy Christian does not seek pain, when it does emerge in life's experiences, it can be viewed not as a random happening, but as within the design of a sovereign, personal God (Rom 8:28).

Why then do Christians succumb to fear, worry and anxiety when God's love and faithfulness are so poignantly communicated in Scripture? Or why would a Christian continue to cling tenaciously to grudges or struggles with personal sin? We find an answer to the paradox in the Bible. Paul tells us in Romans 8:22-24: "We know that the whole creation has been groaning in travail together until now; and not only the creation, but we ourselves, who have the first fruits of the Spirit, groan inwardly as we wait for adoption as sons, the redemption of our bodies. For in this hope we were saved."

God's purpose for each Christian is to conform him or her to the image of his son, Jesus Christ. Although perfection eludes us in this life, this should not keep the Christian from claiming the benefits of that salvation or "wholeness" offered by God through Jesus Christ. Christians need to live in hope, and in the meantime "we all, with unveiled face, beholding the glory of the Lord, are being changed into his likeness from one degree of glory to another; for this comes from the Lord who is the Spirit" (2 Cor 3:18).

So Christians can and do have emotional struggles, but God's offer of salvation is total and involves the well-being of the whole person. God uses the experiences of students to bring about the wholeness he desires. The psychiatric nursing experience can be one of these experiences. Because of the nature of the interaction between nurse and client, the student is afforded a unique opportunity to confront self and grow. There is no equipment or procedure coming between the nurse and the client; therefore the encounter is totally person to person, the self of the nurse with the self of the client. The challenge for the nurse is authenticity, the precursor of which is self-awareness.

Growing in Relationships

Susan was in touch with her beliefs and conflicts as a Christian psychiatric nurse. I found her honesty and courage in articulating them refreshing. Although Susan was assured of God's love and forgiveness on the basis of Scripture and her personal commitment to Jesus Christ, she admitted that she didn't always *feel* loved or free of guilt. "I guess I'm aware of the tension between what I *know* and what I *experience*," she said. Susan's real self was growing through the thoughts and feelings she allowed herself to confront. Sidney Jourard states:

It is not until I am my real self and I act my real self that my real self is in a position to grow. People's selves stop growing when they suppress themselves. Self-alienation tends to make a farce of one's relationships with people.[4]

My colleague and I validated this principle. In our study we learned that there was a significant relationship between the students' awareness of self and the quality of the nurse-patient relationship. A student stated, "I've never learned so much about myself as I have in this psychiatric course." This same student also demonstrated an outstanding nurse-patient relationship. Her openness and honesty elicited a corresponding response in her patient: "I never thought I could tell anyone my real feelings and still have respect for myself." This study validated our hypothesis that two critical processes occur simultaneously in a nurse-patient relationship: (1) as the person develops, the relationship develops; and (2) as the relationship develops, the person develops. The catalytic agent in the relationship is the nurse's self-awareness.[5]

None of us grows in a vacuum; we need each other. I expect to grow as a result of my encounters with students. As an instructor, I also see myself as a motivator of growth. My greatest satisfaction comes from moving the student-teacher relationship past the superficial level to a more substantive level.

One day a student said to me, "You've been a kind of Gibraltar for me through this psych nursing experience." That comment kept me going during an especially trying period. Times of prayer and Bible study have also provided opportunity for intimate understanding, sharing and support in the student-teacher relationship.

During the psychiatric nursing experience, the clinical group can facilitate students' mental and emotional growth by fostering openness and sharing. Janine was extremely quiet in group sessions. It was evident that she had leadership qualities and administrative skills, but she consistently took a passive role whenever opportunities arose for her to contribute. In one of our conferences Janine said that she realized she was not using her gifts because "I'm basically afraid of being criticized, so I just avoid risking it. I'm also afraid of my own rather aggressive tendencies and need to control. I'm not pleased with the way I'm handling these things." Janine asked her clinical group to help her take some risks within the context of her group. The group understood the reason for Janine's reticence and encouraged her to participate.

Students have told me that Bible study and prayer group support, especially during the psychiatric nursing experience, has been of inestimable value. "I hadn't realized how much my Bible study group meant to me," Penny said. "I really needed to be reaffirmed in my belief of God's love and sovereignty when I was being so intensely exposed to hostile and uncontrolled behavior in the clinical setting." She continued, "Our group has become much more open with one another. We realized that we were much more academic than we were intimate in sharing our thoughts." Some excellent materials published by Nurses Christian Fellowship are available for students to use in Bible study or prayer groups.[6]

In our lives there are times when the intensity of our unmet needs can overwhelm us. At such times, professional counseling may expedite emotional growth. Claire was an excellent student and well organized in her personal life. Within a short period of time both her parents died, her boyfriend left her, and she was fired from a part-time job on which she depended. Claire's progressively increasing disorganization and her inability to complete her schoolwork led her to realize her need for professional counseling. As a result she was able to recognize and deal with her anger over feeling abandoned by the significant others in her life. Her festering wounds were aired. She began to progressively understand the nonconstructive force of repressed rage as it related to her recent experiences. She also began to realize the relationship of her recent heavy losses to her increasing disorganization and inability to complete her schoolwork. Through professional counseling, Claire was able to redirect her energies toward growth.

Ellen was a motivated junior student in the psychiatric nursing experience. She began to share some of her developmental background with me. One day she said, "Do you know how I visualize my life?" I assured her that I had no idea. "Like an umbrella," she said, "because it's either up or down." When it was up (which it was for prolonged periods), she said, "I have this dull anxiety that it is bound to fold at some unsuspecting moment. For this reason, even when the umbrella is up, the dread of its possible folding causes me to feel inadequate most of the time."

Ellen's description of her thoughts and behavior suggested that she was dissipating her energies. She knew she was not using her gifts and talents to the extent of her ability. Her interpersonal relationships with family, peers and authority figures had not been at all satisfying to her. Weeks after Ellen had begun to share her thoughts and feelings with me, she very gingerly said, "I guess I never told you that I'm seeing a counselor." She conveyed an attitude of both conviction and apology. I chose to support her on the side of her conviction. "Ellen," I said, "as far as I'm concerned, what you're sharing with me demonstrates another one of your strengths. The commitment to grow toward wholeness is nothing less than strength."

Although the psychiatric nursing experience can arouse doubts and questions for students, it also affords a unique opportunity for growth toward personal wholeness. Self-awareness, which involves honesty, self-disclosure and the acceptance of our vulnerability as human beings, is vital to the process of maturing. In addition, growing as a Christian involves openness and honesty with God. To seek help from others, whether professionals or peers, is not an admission of failure but a commitment to further growth.

Growth is always traumatic because it involves giving up the status quo. The psychiatric nursing experience, with all the anxieties it provokes, can be a time of intense personal and professional growth. Our willingness to accept the challenge determines the extent of our growth.

Notes

Foreword
[1]The working papers, which include a comparison of thirteen psychiatric approaches with Christian beliefs, and the thirteen-page bibliography are available from Nurses Christian Fellowship, 233 Langdon St., Madison, WI 53703.
[2]Journal articles will be listed as they appear in the bibliography available from the NCF office.

Chapter 1: Mental Health: A Personal Struggle
[1]"Spiritual Well-Being," White House Conference on Aging (Washington, D.C.: U.S. Government Printing Office, 1971), p. 1.
[2]Sharon Fish and Judith Allen Shelly, *Spiritual Care: The Nurse's Role* (Downers Grove, Ill.: InterVarsity Press, 1978), p. 39.

Chapter 2: What Is Human? A Context for Defining Mental Health
[1]C. S. Lewis, *The Weight of Glory* (Grand Rapids, Mich.: Eerdmans, 1949), pp. 14-15.
[2]Karl Menninger, M.D., *Whatever Became of Sin?* (New York: Hawthorn Books, 1973).
[3]Jay E. Adams, *Competent to Counsel* (Grand Rapids, Mich.: Baker Book House, 1970), pp. 28-29.
[4]For biblical references, see the following Bible study guides published by Nurses

Christian Fellowship, 233 Langdon St., Madison, WI 53703: *A Lifestyle of Joy, Following the Great Physician, God's Provision for Human Needs, Living in Hope, Mental Health: A Biblical Perspective* and *Studies in Assertiveness.*

[5]Paul Meehl et al., *What, Then, Is Man?* (St. Louis: Concordia, 1958), p. 216.

Chapter 3: Toward a Psychology of Believing

[1]Frank G. Gable, *The Third Force* (New York: Pocket Books, 1970), p. 52.

[2]Abraham Maslow, *Toward a Psychology of Being* (New York: Van Nostrand, 1968), pp. 4, 153, 170, 196.

[3]Carl Rogers, *On Becoming a Person* (Boston: Houghton-Mifflin, 1961), pp. 23, 26-27.

[4]Ibid., p. 7.

[5]Maslow, *Toward a Psychology of Being,* pp. 118, 120.

[6]Abraham Maslow, *Religion, Values and Peak Experiences* (Columbus, Ohio: Ohio State University Press, 1964), p. xiii.

[7]Rogers, *On Becoming a Person,* pp. 344-45.

[8]Ibid., p. 24.

[9]Maslow, *Religion, Values and Peak Experiences.*

Chapter 4: Interpretations of Wholeness

[1]Ranald Macaulay and Jerram Barrs, *Being Human: The Nature of Spiritual Experience* (Downers Grove, Ill.: InterVarsity Press, 1978), pp. 39-40.

[2]Mary Risley, *The House of Healing* (New York: Doubleday, 1961), p. 203.

[3]J. D. Douglas, ed., *The New Bible Dictionary* (Grand Rapids, Mich.: Eerdmans, 1962), p. 1126.

[4]Hans Walter Wolff, *Anthropology of the Old Testament* (Philadelphia: Fortress Press, 1974), pp. 223-29.

[5]David K. Clark, *The Pantheism of Alan Watts* (Downers Grove, Ill.: InterVarsity Press, 1978), p. 42.

[6]Inter-Varsity Christian Fellowship Basis of Faith.

[7]Sandra D. John, personal letter, November 1979.

[8]Patricia McCarty, "Energy: Tapping the Body's Natural Resource," *The American Nurse,* 20 June 1979, p. 8.

[9]Ibid.

[10]Ibid.

[11]Barbara Blattner, *Holistic Nursing* (Englewood Cliffs, N.J.: Prentice-Hall, 1981), pp. 329-30, emphasis added.

[12]Kenneth Pelletier, *Mind as Healer, Mind as Slayer: A Holistic Approach to Preventing Stress Disorders* (New York: Dell Publishing Co., 1977), p. 302.

[13]Brooks Alexander, "Holistic Health from the Inside," *Spiritual Counterfeits Journal,* August 1978, pp. 13-14.

[14]Mark Albrecht and Brooks Alexander, "The Sellout of Science," *Spiritual Counterfeits Journal,* August 1978, pp. 23-24.

[15]Blattner, *Holistic Nursing,* p. 85, emphasis added.

[16]Marilyn Grooms, "Holistic Health. Nursing Fad or Future?" *Texas Nursing,* November/December 1977, p. 12.

[17]Blattner, *Holistic Nursing,* pp. 25, 177.

[18]Roland E. Miller, "Christ the Healer," in *Health and Healing: Ministry of the Church,* ed. Henry L. Lettermann (Chicago: Wheat Ridge Foundation, 1980), pp. 22-23.

Chapter 6: What Are Spiritual Needs?

[1]From a case study by Cheryl Webb.

[2]Adapted from a case study by Ramona Cass.

Chapter 7: Healthy and Unhealthy Religious Beliefs

[1]Wayne E. Oates, *The Religious Care of the Psychiatric Patient* (Philadelphia: Westminster Press, 1978), p. 95.

[2]Wayne E. Oates, *When Religion Gets Sick* (Philadelphia: Westminster Press, 1970), pp. 16-17.

[3]Gordon W. Allport, *The Individual and His Religion* (New York: Macmillan, 1950), p. 78.

[4]J. I. Packer, *Knowing God* (Downers Grove, Ill.: InterVarsity Press, 1973), p. 247.

[5]Oates, *When Religion Gets Sick,* p. 73.

[6]Erik H. Erikson, *Insight and Responsibility* (New York: W. W. Norton, 1964), p. 181.

[7]Oates, *When Religion Gets Sick,* p. 27.

[8]Joseph Cooke, "I Invented an Impossible God," *Eternity,* May 1978, pp. 37-39.

Chapter 8: Assessing Spiritual Needs

[1]Wayne E. Oates, *The Religious Care of the Psychiatric Patient* (Philadelphia: Westminster Press, 1978), pp. 17-26.

[2]Anton Boison, *Out of the Depths* (New York: Harper and Bros., 1960), p. 9.

[3]J. Spencer, "The Mental Health of Jehovah's Witnesses," *British Journal of Psychiatry* 126 (1975):556-59.

[4]Howard J. Clinebell, Jr., *Understanding and Counseling the Alcoholic,* rev. ed. (Nashville: Abingdon Press, 1968), p. 67.

Chapter 9: Meeting Spiritual Needs

[1]Henri Nouwen, *A Cry for Mercy: Prayers from the Genesee* (Garden City, New

York: Doubleday, 1981), p. 174.

Chapter 11: Use of Scripture
[1]Wayne E. Oates, *The Bible in Pastoral Care* (Philadelphia: Westminster Press, 1953), p. 105.
[2]William B. Oglesby, Jr., *Biblical Themes for Pastoral Care* (Nashville: Abingdon, 1980).

Chapter 14: Caring for Your Colleagues
[1]For helpful explanations of the gospel, see: John W. Alexander, *Hope for a Troubled World* (Downers Grove, Ill.: InterVarsity Press, 1978); and Will Metzger, *Tell the Truth* (Downers Grove, Ill.: InterVarsity Press, 1981).

Chapter 15: Are My Beliefs Unbalanced?
[1]William P. Wilson, "Mental Health Benefits of Religious Salvation," *Diseases of the Nervous System* 33 (June 1972):382-86.
[2]Anthony A. Hoekema, *The Christian Looks at Himself* (Grand Rapids, Mich.: Eerdmans, 1975).

Chapter 19: Psychiatric Nursing: An Opportunity for Growth
[1]Diana A. Krikorian and Betty J. Paulanka, "Self-Awareness—The Key to a Successful Nurse-Patient Relationship?" *Journal of Psychosocial Nursing and Mental Health Services* 20 (June 1982):19-20.
[2]V. Parsons and N. Sanford, *Interpersonal Interaction in Nursing* (Menlo Park, Calif.: Addison-Wesley Co., 1979), p. 31.
[3]Nancy Anne Smith, *All I Need Is Love* (Downers Grove, Ill.: InterVarsity Press, 1977), p. 53.
[4]Sidney M. Jourard, "Healthy Personality and Self-Disclosure," *Mental Hygiene* 43 (1959):503.
[5]Krikorian and Paulanka, "Self-Awareness," p. 21.
[6]*Mental Health: A Biblical Perspective* (Nurses Christian Fellowship, 233 Langdon St., Madison, WI 53703) and *Rough Edges* (Downers Grove, Ill.: InterVarsity Press, 1972) are both useful Bible study guides.

Contributors

Mary Berg, B.S.N., is the Southern California area director for Nurses Christian Fellowship and a former nurse on a coronary care unit.

Laura Carlsen is a pseudonym. The author teaches nursing.

Verna J. Carson, M.S.N., is assistant professor at the University of Maryland School of Nursing and has experience in psychiatric nursing and individual and family therapy.

Sandra D. John, R.N., M.S., is a marriage, child and family therapist in Berkeley, California, and a former staff nurse, nursing instructor and chaplain, all in a mental-health setting.

Diana Krikorian, R.N., M.S.Ed., is assistant professor of psychiatric nursing at the University of Delaware and co-coordinator of the Nurses Christian Fellowship Mental Health Task Force.

Sidney Whitley Langston, M.S.N., is clinical administrator with Wycliffe-JAARS and instructor of psychiatric mental health nursing at the University of North Carolina in Charlotte.

Arlene Miller, M.S.N., has taught at Kent State University.

Barbara E. Nelson, R.N., M.S., M.T.S., is nurse-chaplain at the oncology clinic of Boston City Hospital and a doctoral candidate in psychological counseling.

Arlynne Ostlund, B.S.N., is on the staff of Nurses Christian Fellowship in the Chicago area.

Mertie L. Potter, M.S., lectures at St. Anselm College in New Hampshire and is a clinical specialist in psychiatric nursing at a Christian counseling center.

Judith Allen Shelly, B.S.N., M.A.R., is associate director of resource development for Nurses Christian Fellowship and a former staff nurse and family practice nurse. She is also editor of the Spiritual Perspectives in Nursing series listed on page 2.

Kenneth L. Williams, Ph.D., is director of counseling for Wycliffe Bible Translators and a former missionary with Wycliffe.

Subject Index

Scripture Index

The Spiritual Perspectives in Nursing series
edited by Judith Allen Shelly:

☐ *Spiritual Care: The Nurse's Role.* Second edition, revised and enlarged. "[A book for] all those who try to care for the whole person." —*American Journal of Nursing.* Through case studies and practical wisdom, the authors describe how to meet the spiritual needs of sick persons and their families.

☐ *Spiritual Care Workbook.* Nine units of individual and group exercises which apply the principles of spiritual care to practical situations. Units correspond to chapters in *Spiritual Care: The Nurse's Role.*

☐ *Caring in Crisis.* Individual and group studies which provide the biblical basis for spiritual care. Follows the same basic categories as *Spiritual Care: The Nurse's Role.*

☐ *Dilemma: A Nurse's Guide for Making Ethical Decisions.* Text and study guide which provide a practical method for making informed ethical judgments in frequently encountered nursing situations.

☐ *The Spiritual Needs of Children.* Examines the unique spiritual needs of children from a growth-and-development perspective with special application to the health-care setting.

☐ *Spiritual Dimensions of Mental Health.* Looks at spiritual care in a psychiatric/mental health setting and investigates the relationship between spiritual and emotional needs.

The Spiritual Perspectives in Nursing series is sponsored by Nurses Christian Fellowship (NCF), a national ministry which aims to train Christian nursing students and professionals in evangelism, discipleship, missions, and the integration of faith and nursing. NCF also publishes the *Journal of Christian Nursing,* a 32-page quarterly which will help Christian nurses to relate their faith with their profession and to provide spiritual care to their patients. For information about Nurses Christian Fellowship and the *Journal of Christian Nursing,* write 233 Langdon St., Madison, WI 53703.

DATE DUE

NOV 0 7 2011			